WHAT WAS AND IS

WHAT WAS AND IS

FORMAL POETRY AND FREE VERSE

THERESA WERBA

Bardsinger Books
www.bardsinger.com

Books by Theresa Werba

What Was and Is: Formal Poetry and Free Verse
Sonnets
Longer Thoughts
Jesus and Eros: Sonnets, Poems, and Songs
Warning Signs of Abuse: Get Out Early and Stay Free Forever
When Adoption Fails: Abuse, Autism, and the Search for My Identity
Diaper Changes: The Complete Diapering Book and Resource Guide

Upcoming:
Finally Autistic: Finding My Autism Diagnosis as a Middle-Aged Female

Copyright © 2024 Theresa Werba
All rights reserved.

No part of this book may be reproduced, or stored in a retrieval system, or transmitted in any form or by any means, electronic, mechanical, photocopying, recording, or otherwise, without express written permission of the publisher.

ISBN-13: 978-0-9656955-0-3

BARDSINGER BOOKS
www.bardsinger.com
Printed in the United States of America

To my progeny:
Francesca, Angelica, Anthony,
Gloria, Gabriella, Sophia,
Jude, Logan, Theo, Julian,
Rosie, Aria, and Max, and those to follow

PREFACE

This volume of poetry is the distillation of over forty years of writing. There are as many, if not more, poems I have written which are not included as are present here. Most have been previously published, but some are being published here for the first time. I chose to glean what worked thematically as well as musically, to my mind's ear, as a kind of composition in a series of movements, made of individual poems, making up sections, which come together to comprise the whole.

There are eight thematic sections to this work. They represent the areas of interest to me and how best to codify my life experience as it has been expressed through my poetry. There is no reason why one might not begin at any point in the book and read a section that interests them, out of order. Although I assembled the work according to what worked for me logically, and aurally, I hope that the reader will enjoy reading the poetry in any order that will make reading meaningful and rewarding to him or her. The title of each section is a phrase from one of the poems within that section.

I have written in both formal poetry and free verse. The forms include the sonnet—Shakespearean, Petrarchan, Spenserian, hybrid, and a few that don't fall into any specific sonnet category. Other forms include the villanelle, rondeau, ode, pantoum, and nonce forms of my own creation.

In **Writing is the Labor of the Mind,** I delve into the creative process, its joys and frustrations, and my experimentations with and initiation into sonnet forms such the Petrarchan and Spenserian. **All the Loves I've Loved and Known** is a collection of poetry to people I have loved and lost, or whose love I never managed to obtain, throughout my life, and the state of things as it has come to be. **My Mental World is Overloaded** explores various aspects of my own experience with neurodivergence, including Asperger's Syndrome (Level 1 autism), anxiety, and bipolar disorder. **Pantheon** is a collection of poems I have written to, or about, other people— some historical, some contemporary, some literary, some personal. **Music's Made Through It** reflects aspects of my life as a singer and musician. In **The Ebbs and Flows of Life** I bring together poetry about pivotal experiences of my life, such as being adopted, and the finding of both my biological parents. **The Change that Comes with Age** explores the challenges and vicissitudes of the aging process. In **Ever Towards Uncertainty** I try to come to terms with the great changes in my spiritual life over the last few years and where I am at as of the publication of this work.

In 2020 I changed my name to take the last names of both my biological parents, so where I was previously known, and published, under the name Theresa Rodriguez, I am now to be known going forward as Theresa Werba.

As the title suggest, this is a collection of what was, or has been, in my life, and where I am at as of the publication of this work. I truly hope you find the reading of this cumulative collection to be a beautiful and memorable experience.

Theresa Brown Werba
Spring City, Pennsylvania, 2024

CONTENTS

WRITING IS THE LABOR OF THE MIND 13

    The Word-Birth Sonnet 15
    My Journal 16
    Pen to Paper 17
    A Formalist's Delight 18
    Form Sonnet 19
    Sonnet Sonnet 20
    Petrarchan Sonnet 21
    Spenserian Sonnet 22
    Five-Minute Sonnet 23
    Enjambment Sonnet 24
    Couplet Sonnet 25
    A Sonneteer's Musing 26
    Writer's Block 27
    I've never won 28
    The Sonneteer 29
    A Formalist Poet's Lament 30
    Sonnet for the Sonnet-Maker, Edward Oxenford 32
    I straddle worlds 33
    Poetess 34

ALL THE LOVES I'VE LOVED AND KNOWN 35

    For love is pain 37
    Sonnet of the Hardened Heart 38

For what is love?	39
PATRICK	**41**
Finale	43
Calling Day	45
Annelid Sonnet	47
Ten Years	48
Ten Years Ago	49
Fool	50
GEORGE	**51**
I loved you, how I loved you	53
Last night you were alive	54
GABRIEL	**55**
Sweet Bird	57
PAUL	**61**
The Adulterer's Ode, or Song to a Married Man	63
MARLIN	**65**
The Words and the Music	67
Grey Sonnet	69
Shaman of the Waves	70
Platonic Sonnet	72
A body is a shell	73
You've made it clear	74
China Crystal Fairy	75
Oh, when I think back	78
AWILDA	**79**
Awilda Suárez (1979-2011)	81
ANDY	**83**
Venus and Adonis	85
TONY	**89**
For Tony (1960-2017)	91

  You died too soon 92

BERTRAM **93**

  Inside The Hollow Square 95

  Simple Little Thing 96

  I cannot write 97

  Kismet 98

  You were the last 99

CODA **101**

  Oh, would that things were different 103

  They say love 104

  The status of my life 105

  I do not know 106

MY MENTAL WORLD IS OVERLOADED **107**

  Asperger's Speaks 109

  A thousand thoughts 115

  Impatience 116

  For John of the Cross 117

  Cut Sonnet 118

  Dream State 119

  My Bed 121

  The Ability to Forget 123

  To Be, or Not to Be Medicated 125

  You are my better brain 128

  I'm better now 130

PANTHEON **131**

  The Sonnet of JonBenet (1990-1996) 133

  The Trial of Saint Joan of Arc 134

  For Demetra, "of the fruitful soil." 137

  Quasimodo 138

Blessed Margaret Plantagenet Pole (1472-1541) **140**

Martyress Anne Askew (1521- 16 July 1546) **141**

The Earl of Oxenford's Sonnet **143**

Sebastian **144**

The Wise Woman **146**

Maxwell Schollenberger **147**

Goodbye, Sweet Fetal Child **149**

The Ballad of Babi Yar **150**

MUSIC'S MADE THROUGH IT **153**

If I could access **155**

My Piano **156**

Oh, when I hear **157**

Steinway Pantoum **158**

The Sacred Harp **159**

The Neglected Piano **160**

The Classical Singer's Drink Offering **162**

THE EBBS AND FLOWS OF LIFE **165**

If I knew then **167**

Twisted Reckoning **168**

Have I forgotten? **169**

From this tortured bond **170**

These Thirty Years **171**

The Homeless Sonnet **172**

To a dead friendship **173**

An Adoptee's Reflection **174**

What's in a name? **175**

Guard your heart **176**

I am alone **177**

The fallen vestige **178**

THE CHANGE THAT COMES WITH AGE **179**

    The Rise of Fall 181

    I once was sharp as blades 182

    Last Evening's Glance.. 183

    Self-Portrait 185

    What once was is no more 186

    What if my time 187

    Full Circle 188

EVER TOWARDS UNCERTAINTY **191**

    By My Conscience 193

    Oh, what is prayer?.. 194

    To want the things I want 195

    Where is the fire? 196

    The prayers of youth 197

    The simple, stalwart faith 198

    Fool's Wisdom 199

    A Sectarian Sonnet.. 200

    The so-called heathen world... 201

    A Holy Offering 202

    One of the Four Last Things 203

    The Supreme-Breasted One (*El Shaddai*) 205

    Wrong.. 207

    I've said goodbye 209

    Exodus 12 211

    Baruch HaShem (Blessed Be the Name)....................... 212

    So many times 213

ACKNOWLEDGEMENTS **215**

ABOUT THE AUTHOR... **217**

WRITING IS THE LABOR OF THE MIND

The Word-Birth Sonnet

I gave birth to a poem the other day,
I labored for twelve hours in a rhyme,
I centered, conjured, wombed, throbbed, then gave way
To empty out the fullness of my time.

As in the waves and ebbs and flows of life
By blood and pulsing, bearing down its course,
I think, I gestate; for the pangs of strife
Are sperm to my ripe, beating ovoid source.

Oh, I am aching! So intense are all
The squeezings and the earnest tides of pain;
I move about, then settle in to cull
With open heart my brain canal again.

For writing is the labor of the mind;
And I have birthed my children all in kind.

My Journal

Within my world there is a sacred place,
Where I can hide and then reveal my heart;
Where thoughts and feelings go, and become art;
It is a sanctuary, hallowed space.
Creating something new and touched with grace,
I put my mind to pen, and then impart
My soul's outpourings through my mind, to start,
Then show my whole raw self with open face.

And when complete, I then perfect my words,
And get them ready for the world to see;
I take them from these pages, then display
Them out for those who read, and hear. This girds
Me up for naked vulnerability.
Indeed, I offer all I am this way.

Pen to Paper

A sensory experience for me;
A treat for fingers, nose, and ears, and eyes:
It is within the birth of poetry,
The senses help to make the common wise.

For there is beauty where and how I write;
There is a wealth of loveliness in store;
The stirring of my faculties gives sight,
And then I see much more than heretofore.

I feel the paper, smooth, and fresh, and new;
I see the blackness coming from the pen;
I hear the rustling papers that renew;
I smell the pages and the cover again.

My mind creates, and pen to paper be:
I want to touch, and smell, and hear, and see.

A Formalist's Delight

A formalist's delight, it seems to me,
Is placing form and structure above all;
Not given to emotionality,
A thinking thought's perspective overall.

And then there is the verse that is called "free,"
Where everything inside is thus laid bare;
More like a story-telling time to me,
No meter, rhyme or structure anywhere.

But what about a middle way? Wherein
The feelings of the poet are enshrined
By structure and a form, and held within
A better construct, both of heart, and mind?

I want to hear and know a poet's heart,
Not just his head, but both in counterpart!

Form Sonnet

Turn the page and write again today,
Make something come out of an eager mind;
Make something in a new and different way
In something both of earthy and refined.

For when I strive it seems that I can find
What I am looking for in forms like this;
In stricture and in structure there in kind,
Thus, in the freedom that free form can miss.

For freedom in most freedom is remiss
In finding beauty in this poetry;
In building such some scoffers might dismiss:
But such is perfect perfection to me.

And in this challenge offer what I know
In demonstrating where this form can go.

Sonnet Sonnet

To write of love, or speak of other things
Like life or death, or such philosophy
As might stir up an eager mind, which brings
It to a bold, enriched reality:

Oh, perfect, lovely forms! With such delight
The poet and the reader can obtain
A revelation of new thought, in light
Of what the mind on paper may attain.

For Petrarch, Shakespeare, and then Spenser offer
Us cripple-rhythmed beauty in a way
That is uniquely to the point, and suffer
Condensed and distilled thought to have its say.

For I can surely rest my heart upon it:
I love these three forms that are called the sonnet.

Petrarchan Sonnet

A most intimidating form for me,
Because I come to it in ignorance;
And I am hoping that there is a chance
That I can do it justice prudently.
I wish to honor Petrarch cautiously,
Respecting the conventions, if perchance
I can create in noble circumstance
A thing to challenge intellectually.

In all creative bravery I come,
With courage thus in crafting something new;
I push and work and mold, endeavoring,
Producing something then, that can become
So good and lovely, novel, rich and true:
The best that all my faculties can bring.

Spenserian Sonnet

Another form of poetry for me;
Poetic forms concrete, sublime, refined;
Another type of sonnet flowing free;
The product of a careful, studied mind.

In joyous new discovery I find
The puzzle-solving different mental way;
Creative energy will flow in kind
In all that I can do and write and say.

If only every word would thus obey
The many thoughts that full within me spring,
Then I could make a miracle today,
And I would birth again a brand-new thing.

Oh, could I create worthiness in this:
That not one word would here appear amiss.

Five-Minute Sonnet

To write a poem in five minutes today:
Can it be done within this frame of time?
Can there be something I can really say
Within the pulsing meter and the rhyme?

My skill has thus increased, and I am good
At rhyming and at structure at its peak;
I like to say things clearly as I should;
I like to make things lovely as I speak.

For without error I can do it now;
The lines just come so quickly to my mind;
It thus creates a beauty here somehow;
The sweet perfection that I make and find.

But then the final couplet comes and I
Am stuck without an ending, though I try!

Enjambment Sonnet

Stop. And start. Do not be smooth. Create
Some tension. Break it up. Disjoint
Is preferable, with jagged lines. The point
Is to surprise. Surprise! Ha! Then negate
All evenness. It's fun! Don't wait
Upon convention! Do not disappoint
But stretch the rules. Give us a new viewpoint
Or an experiment. Why not? It's great
To be creative. Have more fun! The mind
Deserves some stimulation. Do it! Make
A first-time thing! Be bold with what you find
Inside your thoughts. Think! And then think more. Take
The total of your intellect and share
With gusto something novel, if you dare!

Couplet Sonnet

I wish that I could enter the sublime
And make a special sonnet out of rhyme.

I'd like to take some ordered turns of phrase
And show that I'm observant in my ways.

For I respect the forms of poetry;
Composing works within a boundary.

I love to see what comes of a restriction,
How beauty blossoms from seeds of constriction.

For formless form sometimes lacks discipline;
It often only shows the mood you're in.

The remedy? Endeavor to create
A thing of depth, and breath, and heft, and weight.

For challenges produce in us what's best,
If we can rise to them, and pass the test.

A Sonneteer's Musing

I strive to put my heart and mind to page:
The art of fourteen lines is to be prized;
A craftsman, wordsmith, seeking to engage
The reader, and to be thus recognized.
With blood, and sweat, and tears, works are revised,
And pruned, and honed, in effort to be best;
Of quatrains, couplets, iambs, works comprised
Within the forms of sonnet— best expressed
In all ideas and thoughts within my breast,
And all the turns and lines within my mind.
So, all components here are put to test,
And every facet fits when thus combined.

And for this title I will persevere,
To be known as a bard, a sonneteer.

Writer's Block

I feel like I am plodding through cement;
My mind is full of cotton batting. Dull,
And dense, and empty-headed, thinking spent
On trying to find clarity. To mull
About within and come up vacant. Try
I might but efforts are in vain. My words
Seem plastic, or ephemeral, trite, dry,
No meaning— or I've lost them. All this girds
My faculties to action, but to naught.
I wish I could say what has not been said
Before; but I come up again, distraught
About the product, from a deadened head!

Oh, would that something fresh would come to me,
Not what amounts to sheer banality!

I've never won

I've never won the Poet Laureate,
Nor reached Bestseller at the New York Times;
I haven't earned a Pushcart Prize as yet,
Or garnered First Place for my metered rhymes.

My Twitter following's growing steadily,
(Although I should have started years ago);
My website's just the sort to showcase me,
While Instagram and YouTube help also.

But this I know, that I must persevere,
Because a legacy means the world to me;
Not vain ambition, for I hold this dear:
To be remembered for my poetry.

I'll go from pen, to work, to copyright:
Acknowledged thus, my goal remains in sight.

The Sonneteer

To be acknowledged as a sonneteer,
A craftsman in the art of poetry,
A wordsmith that can write without a peer:
This is the highest goal of all, to me.

I strive, and ache, and push to create more,
And in the three forms I aim to be best;
And offer up from deep within a store
Of fourteen fine lines, in full form expressed.

And after making my initial draft,
I go back and I hone it once again—
And more, and more, until I show a craft
Of sweet perfection, coming from my pen.

For souls to read and listen, this is prized;
But even more that I be recognized.

A Formalist Poet's Lament

It saddens and perplexes me,
The things I hear of late,
Of how to create poetry,
And how to make it "great":

I've heard it's not emotional,
It's nothing how you "feel;"
But it's entirely rational,
Not heartfelt in appeal.

For form and structure matter; I
Agree wholeheartedly;
But that's the point— the heart should try
To speak creatively!

For nature poems are fine and good,
But what about the soul?
Revealing inner workings should
Be every poet's goal!

Why one without the other? Can
There be a compromise?
Amalgamation of the two?
I think it would be wise!

For mind should wed together, meld
With heart to bring around
A fine-fruitioned work, beheld
Where beauty can be found!

For form and structure all alone
Are very often dead;
They need the heart and spirit's groan
To liven them instead!

Though I agree: expression is a
Thing to best proportion;
Too much is out of balance; the
Best overcomes distortion!

I can't and won't extinguish fire
Rising from within;
To temper it is my desire,
A noble discipline!

And so, I ask: why is it best
For one without the other?
To have them both~ this poet's quest,
I will not have another!

Sonnet for the Sonnet-Maker, Edward Oxenford

You know the beats and rhythms, the iamb
Which pulses like a crippled-legged walk;
You, with the force of one who said, "I am
That I am," in iambs you will talk
Of truth and beauty, pain and sorrow, all
And nothing, touching both Heaven and Hell
In what you speak and say, what will recall
The void in the beginning, and will tell
Of voided end, where "Never" ever cries,
And crowns pass to the undeserving fools,
And great men metamorphose into lies,
And there we search and find the hidden jewels.

And there a crown you bear the better part,
In five-beat lines you tell us of your heart.

I straddle worlds

I straddle worlds of possibility,
Between what is not, and what can become;
Across the great divide of what is free
And what is thus constrained by form. At one
With both the fluid, flowing verse which tries
To speak to matters of the heart, and yet
Respecting the conventions which comprise
Through history what we should not forget:
Of structure making wise the commonplace,
And making ordinary the sublime,
And ordering every word with special grace,
And raising verse beyond the realms of time.

I choose to write in ways that come to me:
The Muse's myriad means in poetry.

Poetess

Thinking, feeling, surging, trying,
Contemplating, dreaming, dying,
Resurrecting and creating,
Finding, telling, speculating,
Stretching, seeking, finding, feeding,
Hearing, knowing, testing, bleeding,
Working, laboring, refining,
Learning, editing, defining,
Leaving, tackling, undertaking,
Molding, shaping, breathing, making,
Giving, yearning, hoping, waiting,
Re-revising, loving, hating,
Gelling, setting, and preparing,
Finalizing, sending, sharing,
Publishing, then beaming, grinning,
Crying, celebrating, winning.

ALL THE LOVES I'VE LOVED AND KNOWN

For love is pain

For love is pain: it has to me
been such a fount of misery;
it flows with so much suffering;
a deluge without succoring,
which leaves me in perplexity.

It overwhelms my sanity,
and floods my sensibility;
it drowns my world, enveloping:
for love is pain.

I have not known the mystery
of why this is my destiny.
It causes all my wonderings,
my questions, and my ponderings,
the waters of my agony:
for love is pain.

Sonnet of the Hardened Heart

Care less, I warn myself; bother no more
With inner crevices: prying the shell
Like scabs (rough, oozing, sore), which crust, but tell
Of tumults against the psychic seabed floor;
It is in vain. Swollen and hard around
The meat (like newborn skin, or the vaginal flower),
The protection, obdurate, damns me. Damn the mound
Which buries my soul and suffocates what little power
My will may afford. That meat, that flower, that skin
(A pulsing pinkish mass) is thus entombed;
And yet, for her to exist at all, the wound
Must needs be sealed by this guardian within.

She lives within her shell; perhaps she dies
As well, because it makes and mutes her cries.

For what is love?

For what is love? Is it a mystery,
A surge of chemicals within the mind?
Is it a chain reaction, fervently
Cascading urge and thought into a bind?

Is love always forever? Must it last
Throughout the varied courses of all time?
Or can it ebb and pass away, as past
Old passions fade from flowerings of our prime?

For love may seem like an eternity,
A never-ending state; but even this
Can end, as best intentions passionately
Declare what once was true is now amiss.

For love may seem eternal at the start,
But even love dies from a dying heart.

PATRICK

Finale

The rigor mortis of my love for you
has not yet set in.
Yes, I have plucked you out, bad eye, bad tongue—
offending me even yet; bad flora.
You seat yourself inside my open wound, virulent
pathogen, leaving me but to ooze,
and scab, and crust.

And then, your repeated exacerbations
cause my worn flesh to swell once more—
it feels like pinpricks, scraping the inside
of my ulcerated place.

(Unseen chemistry reacts with every
meeting; are you so oblivious to it?)

And yes, slave driver, you hold me in your
unseen chains,
while you call me quaint, a relic of
mistakes; bringing me to the
platform to display or sell at will.

And of my nature, I delight in even
that chain that seems to bind me!
With each yearning, the yoke tightens— more abrasions—
as you chat about my insufficiency
to buyers or viewers.

And why, as I touch my neck,
do I feel the binding chain,
but as you look to me, none appears?
Any why, as the ulcer, marred by
overgrowth, infection, grows into a
reddened flower— a rose,
do you not even stop to pick or smell,
or notice your noble offspring, bleeding bright?

Indeed, into hell-fire I have already been cast:
Cheyne-Stokes almost ceased; the body
jerks in last
attempt.

Calling Day

(To the tune of "At Seventeen" by Janis Ian
Solo voice, acoustic guitar, alto saxophone, double bass, Jazz drums, maracas)

I learned my fate on Calling Day
You said your love had died away
Our love of thirty years was gone
My heart became a vagabond

You threw it, beating, all away
And your sweet words you could not say
For now they just were fantasies
That you hoped were fulfilled by me

But then I'd changed too much to take it
Before this, you had grown to fake it
Inventing love you did not feel
In hearts I swore were fully sealed
And called by God to marry now
Relying on the Larchmont vows
We said so many years ago
But suddenly you now let go
Of all that was so real
—on Calling Day

And now, my life's about to end
You will not even be my friend
My "caretaker" you will not be
You had your lover fantasy

But now, you cast me far away
I need you most in every way
In body, mind, in soul, and heart
But you just wish me to depart

*We shared our hearts, our body love
And at one time, even God above
But now, in your simplicity
You reject my complexity
And turn to your compliant bird
The Raven whom you've seen and heard
You feel's a better fit than me
You seek to go out easily
And leave the pain to me
—on Calling Day*

*I die today, tomorrow too
I die from all my love for you
A love I did not give away
Or let die with a rainy day
I loved you since the day we met
A marriage for us to happen yet
In life that was to come to be
Not right away; eventually*

*But somehow even with the joy
Of reunion, I was just a toy
You never told the truth to me
But used me and then abused me
Used words you never meant to live
And closed a heart you did not give
You took back what you gave to me
And left me broken and empty
Tears in memories
—on Calling Day*

Annelid Sonnet

An annelid is a blood-sucking creature, like a leech

I thought I had forgotten you by now,
But I have not. Must I go again
Into this place of torment? Tell me how
To get rid of this leech that suckles when
I try to free it. How I can I walk on
When I am chained? I bury you inside,
Outside, within, withal, whereon, be gone!
Be dead! But in the casket you abide,
Alive but molded, withered; rotten worm
That will not die, though I had thought you dead!
I lunge forth and away but you hold firm
With prongs embedded in my bones and head.

Oh, you have held a place within too long,
Too undeserved, too late to right the wrong.

Ten Years

Ten years it's been since I have seen your face,
Looked in your eyes, or having heard your voice;
Ten years since I have known your warm embrace,
Before you cast me out, by callous choice.

Ten years ago I loved you, oh, so well,
You were my world, yet wanted to be free;
Ten years ago you had me in your spell,
But then you turned away, rejecting me.

In these ten years I've learned to let you go;
I've learned your love and mine were not complete;
I've learned as I grow older, this I know:
I've learned to take the bitter with the sweet.

And as my hair has turned from brown to grey,
I love you not as I did yesterday.

Ten Years Ago

Ten years ago I last looked in your eyes,
So beautiful and blue, so clear, so bright;
I was so happy to be in your light,
But darkness came; you took me by surprise.
Ten years ago, indeed, I was unwise—
Perhaps a lack of vision and insight;
Because you caused the day to become night,
And shut out all my tears, and pains, and cries.

In ten long years the sun will shine again,
Although the clouds do cover me around;
Though I have wondered if a better way
Would ever come to me; oh, if and when
A shining strength of liberty be found.
It's coming: I await the effulgent day.

Fool

Fool that I was, oh fool, I was a fool,
That I had ever opened up my heart
And let you, rogue, into it. Not a part
Of me escaped humiliation. Cruel
As cruelty can be, you were the tool
That sunk my spirit; you deigned to impart
That lasting blow to keep us both apart,
Exposing my full self to ridicule.

For if indeed I had had better sense
Than fall for such a piece of work as you,
When everything I did was an offense,
And your supposed false love was never true,
Oh, had I had the sense I do today,
I could have wisely sensed to run away!

GEORGE

I loved you, how I loved you
To George Cabral (1948-1995)

I loved you, how I loved you in those days:
The truth that was within you as you'd speak;
I loved how you were strong when you were weak;
I loved how you loved God in all your ways.
You gave the Lord all laud, and thanks, and praise,
And all your worship-fullness was unique;
I loved your spirit's voice~ bold, fresh, yet meek,
And "Never Give Up!" was your trademark phrase.

But then the evil, dying sickness came
That was to separate our everything;
And then I searched in others for the same
Pure, humble spirit from your heart's wellspring.
But they were each a substitute that lied,
Because I still did love you when you died.

Last night you were alive

Last night you were alive, alive, it seems,
And too good to be true, for you were here;
But only in the phantoms of my dreams,
For there I touched you, kissed you, held you near.

Alive you were, as if you were not dead,
I felt your skin, your body, saw your face,
I looked into your eyes~ so much unsaid
In memories devoid of time and space.

And then I felt alive! Yes, I could feel
As I did all those many years ago,
When you and I had love, unreal to real:
I'll dwell in sleep, and daily life forgo.

Last night was always, now, and yesterday;
Abide, phantasm: succour me, I pray.

GABRIEL

Sweet Bird

I looked up
the first time you flittered past me.
"Sweet bird," I thought,
"he soars so gracefully."
It was still summer,
and we both took in
what air and heat and light
were left to us.
You, above my head,
about my eyes,
charming me with
your colors, your wings,
and your voice.
My ears began to itch
to hear you chirp
each time your flight
would intersect the spot
where I sat.
It was a treat
to be busy in my work
or thought
to suddenly see you
perched nearby.

"Poor thing," I mused,
"he must be hungry.
Look how he hovers about me.
How does he know
I have anything to feed him?"
(For when you arrived

I know why you were cooing.
A little bit of bread,
and someone to hear
your melodies, perhaps)

So within the wrappings of
my bosom
I pulled out the bit of
nourishment
which I tucked away
and kept to feed the birds
if one should ever approach.
I tossed it in chunks
and crumbs fell about
the ground.
I watched as you swooped down
and, tentatively,
began to peck at the farthest edge of earth
where the bread lay, strewn.
"*Sweet little bird,*" I thought,
"*he's frightened. Does he think I mean
to scare him away?*"

I watched on the edge of the bench,
wondering if you would indeed
reach in and eat.
You did, but grabbing a chunk in your little beak,
you quickly flew away,
leaving me to gather up
the many crumbs
you left behind.

This I did,

and hid the little packet
again
in the many layers of my bosom.
And yet,
how I had longed
for you to stay
only a moment longer,
for me to hold out my finger,
and you could leap onto it,
so I could stroke you.

And now, with the coming spring sun,
I sit in the breeze,
hearing chirps and tweets
again.
I look up
and catch you flittering past,
watching as you ascend and soar and glide,
overhearing now and then
a melody.
I watch
as you pick
about the benches
for crumbs and crusts.

And so I sigh,
and opening my wrappings,
once again
I spill
crusts and crumbs
upon the greening, yearning earth,
awaiting your long descent.

PAUL

The Adulterer's Ode, or Song to a Married Man
(6/8 for solo voice and acoustic guitar)

The inspiration for this ode
is timeworn and well known:
we bear the product of our acts;
we reap what we have sown

You touched inertia in my heart
and song the ache became—
from heart, to mind, to paper, to voice
and back to heart again:

You then fell in my open void
and made me come alive—
is it because I've starved so long
that now I'm satisfied?

And yet, the ache continues, or
is deeper than before;
because I know you are not mine,
I cannot have you more

But then I dream of you and I,
another time and place
the "what if's," "should have beens," and "whys,"
and present life effaced

Oh, why are we so foolish
to induce forbidden fire,
when all that comes is misery,
frustration and desire?

MARLIN

The Words and the Music

I neared the casket or the grave
given up for dead,
and then the music that you gave
resurrected me.

Oh, not of earth, or even flesh
but mind and heart instead—
this simple contact, new and fresh
unsettles me.

Disparate lives, two worlds apart
though sometimes joined in song,
or keys, or pipes played, sound near heart,
It cannot be!

The song within me aches— my voice,
deferred in hope, but strong—
to make such music is my choice:
How can it be?

A tender wafting in my sight
like incense smoke, uncurled:
perhaps two disjoint strands unite
in fleeting camaraderie.

Oh, can you be a soulmate? Dare
enjoin my distant world?
Though I am bound, are you aware
of change to me?

Oh, dear musician, literate one,
who loves both sound and mind,
see what this loneliness has done?
I yearn in me.

Though full surrounded now— at bay,
I find you more than kind:
a kindred heart; then yearn the day
when I am free.

Grey Sonnet

You say that you are grey, but do you know
How shades of grey are complementary
To russet, red, maroon, or crimson's flow
And other hues of blood that bleed from me?

You admix, so you say, of black and white;
But did you notice how the dawn of grey
Will burst with yellow purples, pinks and light
When face to face confronted with the day?

Then you are every color and are none:
For black absorbs and white reflects; yet free
In alchemy the rigid comes undone,
And then my spectrum you more clearly see.

For grey to dwell alone is grey indeed
When colors yearn to contrast, blend, and bleed.

Shaman of the Waves

I am the raging tempest tossed
upon the fretful sea;
you are the calm and quiet gale
that steadies me.

And yet I am the raging sea
as well as all its roar;
and you are even, still, the sure
that calms the shore.

And I am blackened night as when
the ship has sunk away;
and then I see your light which shines
as if a day.

And in the dark and cold, alone
I cry for one to hear,
and then you come; you are the lifeboat
drawing near.

This vessel that you are is strong
to bear all my within,
for you receive the charge with grace
and take me in.

You tilt against the whirling swirl
and navigate the course
so far from tumult, where I dwell
with ever force.

Your shoulder is against the gale
and me against your chest,
and we against the hollow grey
I come to rest.

I find mercurial repose
upon a curious shore;
because you gently landed me,
I ask no more.

And so we are of polar force
that meets in synergy:
you are the shaman of the waves;
I am the sea.

Platonic Sonnet

Sweet succor! sweet relief! a moment here,
A moment there, the precious hour that fades
Into a wisp of time too soon, so dear!
Our fleeting meeting of the mind invades
My depth and breathing. But I try to stay
Away. I fear that you would fear me. I
Am not easy; this I know. I stray
At being at ease or at calm. I try;
I do; I don't; I do not call; I call,
But then I wait a long time between more.
I hope that by a deprivation all
Might turn into a longing at your core.

But then I think that Plato might be true:
Obliterating carnal love for you.

A body is a shell

A body is a shell, a case, a packaging in time,
Vulnerable to decay, touched by both cruel and the sublime,
While housing greater portions of our being than we see;
The body blinds us both to God and our humanity.

Within this mass of blood and flesh and pulsing is much more
Than what is seen; two thirds of what we are, the very core
Of our being is beyond this place: spirit and soul
Complete the human triumvirate: the parts reflect the whole.

It is not mere body of the earth that drew my heart to you.
Your better self, your spirit and your soul had touched me through
To my inner being, calling deep beyond this earthly space
To commune where body and gender ever fail to stake a place.

You seek a form, a kind of body; but yet, is not love
The thing you really seek? A perfect tenderness above
The pullings and the urges that fulfill, then fall apart?
I may not be the body you seek, but seek within my heart:

For within the confines of tears and fears and yearnings I can be
The love you seek; in truth, the very person who can free
You from the yearning to be loved. And well: because I do
Already love you; for so long I have dearly loved you.

You've made it clear

You've made it clear that you've rejected me;
I've offered all my heart and soul to you;
I've stayed the person that I have to be,
And yes, I do remain hard, fast and true;

I know that love is never made by force;
I know that when you love it must be free;
But curious is the fact you've been the source
Of so much angst, and hurt, and pain, to me.

I cannot change the choices of your heart,
Or force a change where choice is never free;
Your stern directive forces us apart,
So adamantly you have turned from me.

For though I've longed for you in every way,
I also love enough to stay away.

China Crystal Fairy

That fragile crystal China winged thing,
that delicate fairy creature with rainbows and polished beauty,
how I held it in my hands as if it were a hummingbird
only to realize my heavy hands had crushed it
and it lay in pieces in broken bits and then my hands bled.

The spirit of that firefly hastened away and I had prisms mixed with blood.

I tried to see if I could somehow put the pieces back together but there was
not enough glue in the world to do it
and my glue was too strong and dense for its fine form.

I could have had a room full of these dripping winged treasures and made a chandelier so bright my heart would have never needed another light.

I saw the colors and I saw the white light and in that was beauty and truth.

If I had kept the figurine in its case, it would be there still, I could see it and see the rainbows that it made when the sun would hit its smoothness.
But now the broken pieces go back on the shelf without a remedy.

My tears would not be glue strong enough to beckon the spirit of the fairy back to me.

I loved its beauty so much that I broke it, loving it so hard.
My hands desired what they could not have,
And now I clasp blood and slivers of what remains.

Oh, come back to me, crystal fairy, come back! But what remains is the twilight of the light that passed by when you left your body behind in my hands.

I rub the slivers deeper as my hands wring in repentance and grief,
tears and blood,
looking for your flight of fancy to come back,
nighttime firefly.

But even if you could somehow embody that crystal light again,
I am sure my hands would be no less obtuse or crude
and once again I would snap and break you
and you would have to fly again away
to the world of spirits.

All I have to offer are the hands bloodied by your crystal carcass
and the tears of losing you
to beckon your return.

But it is not possible
because I snapped and crushed your delicate form in my zealous and clumsy hands
and there is not another one for you to inhabit again.

Firefly, good night! and firefly,
in the dark and dreams you may come by and your wings once more
show your rainbow prism lights to me,
but only in dreams and only in day dreams.

I wish I had had the hands of a princess and not a clod,
of an angel and not of dirt and mud
but now you belong to them
and not my hopes or how I dream or what I dream.

Sing and play among the fairies and cupids and angels and butterflies
because I sit down and hang my head
in my own bloodied hands
with nothing more than memories
and tears
and the drippings of what remains

The admixture of what was once

what you are
and what is no more
between my palms.

Oh, when I think back

Oh, when I think back to those halcyon days,
When I believed the possibility
That truest love would manifest to me
And highest hopes would set the heart ablaze,
I looked amidst the heat, and smoke, and haze
To find this source of reciprocity,
To find the embers, glowing earnestly
Which gave me joy, but it was not to be.
For passion only came from in my heart
And not another, for it was not you
Who loved me back, but bid me to depart,
And stomped upon the yearning fires, too.
For all my dreams were thus deludedly
The conflagrations of a fantasy.

AWILDA

Awilda Suárez (1979-2011)

I could have loved you. Then you offed your body,
But not your soul and spirit. Oh, dear one,
Whom I could have held and helped, your sprightly-
Minded, tender heart was stretched and spun
To be a compliment to mine, like two
Among a sea of many. In the time
Of our derangement I had found you true
And earnest, wanting, hoping to align
Yourself to me. We almost made a home
Together; what if we had done it? Could
This act have saved you? In a poem
You spoke as I speak, but you should
Be speaking still. And now without you here
I realize my inaction cost you dear.

ANDY

Venus and Adonis

I see her standing there.
Ringlets of curls cascading down
Soft shoulders
Onto the copious breasts of pearl and alabaster.
The curls unfurl longer and longer,
Shining and reflecting like circle rings
The sun which hits them.

She walks, tall. Her feet bare and white,
Painted with lilies and grass.

The mountains in front of her
Are billows of soft escape,
And how I wish I could
Bury myself in them,
Taste and touch them,
Suckle them and know them,
Honor them and find them
Again and again.

Escape into her forest
Where rivers flow
Of sweetness and fruit
Between everything and everywhere.
She is the entity, the beauty,
The thing of dreams.

Her eyes are mine, I see her like me,
Blue and green gemstones
A face of chisels and a nose of royalty,
Chin proud and pointed
As fitting the princess of my dreams.

If I could hold her waist and draw her near
I could wrap its narrow shape around my arms
Into rounding hips which make their way

To gardens and forests.
And there I could die in peace,
Forever.

And then you.
The straight and narrow.
You came from the waves,
Unexpectedly,
Startling my gaze,
Seeking my devotion,
As a jealous god.
Adonis coming forth
To come.
Walking tall against the blue and waves,
A face painted and made in stone
Since there was a way to make a man a god.
The sun backs aside
To honor your glistening.
My breath gives pause
To the beating in your chest,
What seeks to mount and conquer
With the force of thrust.
I comply in reverence and fear,
Helpless to overcome
Helpless not to come.

To project and to push you come
At me
Your face of a god and form of a god,
Full phallus of force,
Fine and perfect strong.
Of every dream into a face,
Of every yearning into your arms.
A statue has become a man,
The man a dream,
The dream to me.
And for a moment I am one
With the body of a god
In your embrace.

I taste your lips
And you attempt to circle me,
I examine them with my own.
As my tongue gets to know yours,
As I swell with fear and unexpecting.
For a moment I have known
What it is to worship a god.

And then I see your eyes look up
And her, beyond me,
And I see her, too.

Her sterner eyes do not submit
To stuff of darks and smalls
Encroaching on her bright territory.
My eyes greet hers
But turn away,
Ashamed that my shadow touched your form
Even for a moment
In the face of her jealous eyes.
She asks for you
But I remember my goddess
And I seek her, too,
And ask for an audience,
If she would condescend
A moment of her beauty
To soothe me before
Beckoning you away
Forever.

Together we turn
To her feet
And seek to climb her
As you walk away
From my selfsame eyes
Into her billows and her hair.
Such is the truth of worship
Of the goddess

And she beckons us both
To come to her,
But not you to me
Again.

I turn in reverence,
And love her, too.
Her right of power,
Accepting the greater decree
Of her beckoning arms.
You go, then I.
Together we search her,
But you may find her.

And I may yearn alone
At a distance,
Forever,
While you conquer
In victory
Her perfect everything,
Again, and again, and again,
And together you both bid me
Go away,
My eyes to the ground
Dropping salt tears
As I glance back
One more time
At the two of you
Laughing in delight
At victory of the chase
And conquest
As I walk away.

So I release you to her form
And function
For she is mine,
More beautiful,
Enshrined in pillows,
Awaiting us both.

TONY

For Tony (1960-2017)

And now the time comes: I must say goodbye.
Goodbye to you in body, soul and mind;
The tears don't come, I don't weep, I don't cry,
And yet I mourn for sorrow that I find.

Goodbye to all we shared in old times past;
Goodbye to all the future laid ahead;
But memories remain, in lifetime last;
I say goodbye to bury them instead.

Goodbye to dreams and hopes, a future here;
Goodbye to things ahead that never came;
Goodbye because to many you were dear;
And things will never, ever be the same.

So even if my eyes are clear and dry,
I mourn for you, although I cannot cry.

You died too soon

You died too soon; too young for them and me.
It comes in waves, the ebb and flowing tear;
I feel your absence ever presently.

They think of you so reminiscently,
And memories of fading yesteryear.
You died too soon; too young for them and me,

And thinking of what was, what is, will be,
The apparitions of your life appear.
I feel your absence ever presently

For in the mind is what the heart can see,
And then these images all disappear.
They died too soon; too young for them and me.

And then again you come in memory—
Your voice, the shadows of your body near.
I feel your absence ever presently,

And then again the visages will flee
And fuzzy recollections become clear.
You died too soon; too young for them and me:
I feel your absence ever presently.

BERTRAM

Inside The Hollow Square

It is a moment or a spot in time,
When time is quieted and put away;
A simple thing becoming the sublime,
Suspended and eternal in a day.

And all around me just dissolves to naught;
I feel my world around me disappears;
It is just me before you— I am caught
Between my happiness and many fears.

You look at me as if you've known before
All that I am in heart and soul and mind,
Or wish to know them, here and now and more:
These gazes that reveal and seek entwined.

For then I look up and I realize
I get lost when I look into your eyes.

Simple Little Thing

It really is a simple little thing,
The insignificance of it, not much;
But what reactions can an action bring—
The magic of your brief, ephemeral touch?

Are you aware of what you do to me?
The soft engendering in a caress?
Do you have any sense of what can be
Within a body touched by loneliness?

For your warm hand thus permeates my skin;
My heart responds in reciprocity;
It stirs all kinds of fantasies within;
My innards pondering what things might be.

Perhaps it isn't really what it seems,
And this is all the product of my dreams.

I cannot write

I cannot write of what can never be,
Of what I cannot have, though I can dream;
I cannot write about inside of me
Of what imaginings can make, and seem.

For it can seem a true reality
Where I can come to tell you how I feel,
Where I see you and you in turn see me,
And all I ruminate about is real.

But then I wake up from the sleepless state,
And realize it all was in my mind;
The rich and raw and beautiful is fate
That never comes to me, for me to find.

Oh, how I wish sometimes I would not wake,
So that I could one moment more partake.

Kismet

If I'd been younger, or you not so old,
Or we'd met at a different time and place,
Would there have been within your heart a space
For me, for love to reach and grab ahold?
Might there have been such glories to behold
As two might have when two are given grace
To become one? Might destiny erase
The present and allow dreams to unfold?

For here I am and there you are. And we
Are not together, for I see within
My mind's eye something like the rolling sea
Lapping up against the shore, akin
To union that will never, ever be,
As un-united as it's always been.

You were the last

You were the last; there won't be any more.
My heart, no longer pliable, is set;
Like adamantine to a liquid core
I stand impervious, without regret.

Each of the loves and lovers of the past
Once burned within me, making heat and fire,
But wafting vapor-smoke will never last:
Hot memories of longing and desire.

My single, final hope: I thought perhaps
There might have been a future; but I see
How thoroughly delusion so entraps:
It was a sad, pathetic fantasy.

You die away: I do not cry, or sigh,
Or say goodbye, or try to wonder why.

CODA

Oh, would that things were different

Oh, would that things were different than they are,
And love and longing weren't intertwined
And I had one without the other. Far
From this would better be the place of mind
Where health and wholeness dwells. Instead for me
I have what seems a knack for true illusion
And I am stuck within a fantasy
Which grows into a much bigger delusion.
I wish that maybe someday there would be
An actuality to what's my muse
Instead of dreams and figures. Oh, to see
Reality that I would fear to lose!

Perhaps the day will come, but until then
I wait for future: if, and why, and when.

They say love

They say love cannot die, but you can kill it,
though ruminating promises were made;
because it is expedient to will it
dead and gone, when hopes are not allayed!

So put an end to it. Go, terminate
these inner machinations. Is it aught,
the better thing to die than germinate
futility? Behold, what love has wrought!

For seed like this can grow into a weed
that chokes out thoughtful prudence. Therefore, cease
the striving. Sproutings from that little seed
will only serve to fester an increase!

Because love needs to be thus decimated,
Especially when not reciprocated!

The status of my life

The status of my life is such that I
Have tried to love with all my will and heart;
But now that love is over, I will try
To lay down shoulds and should-have-beens apart.

This place is sacred and unseen, I start
A new thing in this curious, hidden way;
Another level entity, in part
Of future's every moment, come what may.

For this is new, a dawning of the day,
Where memories and dreams will never go,
Where past's great triumphs now will never stay,
With future disappointments hurting so.

So even when it empty comes to me,
I unentangled would prefer to be.

I do not know

I do not know what love is any more.
I do not understand my present state.
From memories emanating from the core
Of my whole being, this I contemplate.

The pain, the hurt, rejection, questionings
Why my particular fate has come to me;
Why others have what I do not, which brings
About a sense of perverse destiny.

For this I know, that I have loved, and tried,
And tried, and tried, but efforts were in vain;
I know that something deep within has died,
And I shall never get it back again.

And yet, I plod ahead, myself, alone;
And think of all the loves I've loved and known.

MY MENTAL WORLD IS OVERLOADED

Asperger's Speaks

Asperger Syndrome was reclassified as Autism Level 1, part of Autism Spectrum Disorder, in the DSM-5 (2013).

In a world of hyper-stimuli,
Lights and sounds and touches,
I retreat into the world within myself
for relief.

There is too much to process
all at once,
It comes at me like a screaming hoard,
shoving up against my walls
and forcing me to interact.

Why interact? Most talk like that is
stupid, pointless, irrational.
*If you do not care how I am today,
why do you ask me how I am? Just say
Good Morning or Hello!*

It is this stupid, slow world,
Where I move faster, think better,
process factually,
that frustrates me.

*And when you talk, do I
really understand? Why is it
that we misalign, why do
I misperceive what you are saying?
Is this why you are frustrated
with me?*

Why is my voice too loud,
my speech too intense?
Why do you think I'm being rude,
when I am just annoyed?

You do not like the things I like,
the things that interest me,
and I could talk unimpeded
for hours about these
very interesting things
unless you stopped me.

It could be canals, or the Shakespearean authorship issue,
or points of linguistics,
or the study of late Antiquity, or Jewish history,
or poetry— my poetry.

You do not understand the tiny things
that matter so much to me, or why they do,
why I must tell you every detail,
every minutiae, why I have to explain,
must explain
everything, every little thing.

My mental world is overloaded and then
I go outside where the world
is overloaded and then
I can do no more.

At times it seems I do not even care
because in that moment it is simply
not available for me to care.

But inside myself, my heart
is wide, and deep,
so deep I have to shut it off
in order to get through the
interactions into which
I must engage.

*Why has it been so hard
to walk into a store,
or interact in public?*

*Must I always play the game,
must I always act, pretend,
and be somebody else
just to buy something?*

My mind explodes
with ideas, thoughts,
learning and logic,
connections and observations,
but when to stop, and when to give you
a turn to speak
evades me.

I am learning to do this to this very day.

Without the social mask, I'm sure
you would not like me;
being myself is one long conversation
with myself.

But I have learned to smile,
to look into your eyes,
to be politic when necessary
(though I hate necessity),
to play the nice game of
interaction.

If you would only understand!
My heart is not my
talking, but I am truly
trying to reach you through my
talking, and so I'm talking,
on and on and on and on and on.

For rages come, and anger,
the cursing, the frustrations,
the rantings.
Why is everyone so stupid?
Why am I in a world of idiots?
Why doesn't this person
have a brain?

Perhaps my only disability
is my intelligence.
My hyper-wired brain
is both an advantage
and a defect.

Rigid and inflexible to sudden change,
it sends me into spasms
as I try to figure out what
is now going on.
But it is not supposed to be this way!

That's not what the menu said!
That's not what you told me before!

What I cannot process I therefore cannot understand,
And the world then makes me angry
and frustrated.

Only in the confines and restrictions
of my bed, my routine morning puzzles,
my daily evening internet,
am I at equilibrium.

Here it is I can find the quiet
absent within my own mind.

So when I talk, that is truly me,
trying to get out, one iota of the cosmos
within, one speck of the vast
universe of my thoughts.

Wouldn't you like to join this world and
listen for a little while?

So, be patient with me, try to listen through,
try to understand,
because inside I am very, very alone,
just my thoughts and me,
trying to be heard.

High Anxiety

Oh, come and view the workings of an over-anxious mind,
The day-to-day of black, cold darkness that can paralyze;
So full of hidden terrors and foreboding that in kind
I wonder what catastrophe might soon materialize.

For wakeful nights keep sleep away with worry and with dread;
A feeling of impending doom that flutters in my heart;
I fight in vain to overcome the unknown, but instead
I lie awake and wish this apprehension would depart!

This is a covert, secret place unseen by outside eyes;
I wear a coating of some calm to masquerade the fear,
And try to cloak, conceal away; but then I realize
I am an open book and my proclivities are clear!

What horrors I invent! What terrors and calamity!
And yes, worst-case scenarios are ever festering;
For when the palpitations come, I wish that I could see
A better situation than what I'm engendering.

Instead, I quiver and in trepidation I can quake
In endless combinations of my mental wonderings;
Distortion causes all my equilibrium to shake,
Because I cannot cease from such tumultuous ponderings!

What would it be, if somehow I could live without this weight,
And future tense would only be a present tense to me;
Oh, then I could live in the moment, in this pleasant state,
And be completely free from all this high anxiety!

A thousand thoughts

A thousand thoughts I cannot seem to shake;
a whirlwind of pressure in my head;
I wish I had a stronger faith, instead
of worrying of all that is at stake.
I wish that with this energy I'd make
a place where I no longer fear or dread,
(the possibility I could be dead);
I do not sleep well but I lie awake.

But I must face what possibility
awaits me as I sit and wait and ponder,
and try to put these anxious thoughts away
and hope that time is time given to me,
and I can live my life, and not to wonder
if I will get to live another day.

Impatience

I wait without relief here for this thing that I desire,
I hold my inner breath and then I breathe out once again;
I feel the jitters jittering and wish I could acquire
a better state of being than to wonder "where?" and "when?"

My blood gets hot and bothered by this endless waiting game;
I sit and try to feel some calm, but always in my mind
is what I am still waiting for~ it's ever and the same,
again and over once again, the stress is unconfined.

Oh, when will it be over and I have this thing at last?
When will I put it out of mind? When shall I be released?
When will this longing meet its resolution, and be past
its climax, and the afterglow, and all my worry ceased?

Oh, I'm not happy here at all in this, my present state:
I need to take my mental medicine, relax, and simply wait!

For John of the Cross

16th century mystic John of the Cross (1542-1591) is the author of The Dark Night of the Soul.

It was five years of darkness. I was dead
But barely breathing, living hardly; lain
About the marble slab. It was my bed
Where I would live, if life were sleep. Heart slain
Of all feeling— empty, absent, gone—
Was beating only, but no heart therein.
I labored on like vapors, still upon
A dark moor. Festered nothing was my sin,
If it was sin; in truth I do not know
The reason for so long an empty shell.
My walking form lacked why or where to go;
This surely was an earthly form of hell.

I yearned for health and wellness, to be whole,
But I was in the dark night of the soul.

Cut Sonnet

What will begin as thought will end in deed.
A striking of the skin of flesh and heart
And then the friction giving way to bleed
With red relief, like tears which know no part
Of reason or of sanity, but flow
Responsive to the need to rip and see
A mirror wounding from without. Although
One can touch, the other is not free—
Except in reciprocity, to splay
Itself, the earthly to the earth.
And then this ugly skin-ding will display
Until the salve of time will show its worth.

For memories can thus become unmade,
And pain can ease and even scars do fade.

Dream State

I woke but I was not awake. Around
Me was a canyon— grave-like, dark abode
Where light was dim and dying. And the sound

About me echoed breath. The night bestowed
Around me festering, thick, fetid air,
Cold and black. This closed space did forebode

Forthcoming unknown states, and places where
I had to stay silent. But then the descent,
Descending in a spiral in midair

Which caused my senses to disorient.
I then could taste of death, an acrid taste,
Displeasure adding to my discontent

Where whirling down and nausea interlaced;
And then I stopped. By then I could not feel
A thing. For numbness somehow had replaced

My sense of touch. My fingers, dead, unreal,
Like phantoms had no body. All I'd known
I knew no more. And throughout this ordeal

I could touch no one. I was all alone
In this dark, blinded world— I could not see
As well, the absence of the light so shown

In this weird, womblike state, which was to me
A mummy, or a corpse. Was I alive?
Was this a wrapped cocoon? Then suddenly

It felt like birthing. When I did survive
The squeezings and the movement, water broke
Around me. Then my senses did revive

As I emerged. What thoughts did this evoke,
Feeling new, delivered? Was I free,
Or was this just a dream as I awoke?

No matter what, my sensibilities
Were shattered by this psychic fantasy!

My Bed

When life has burdened me and robbed me of an easy way,
I've looked for succor, such as one can access every day;
A simple, sweet solution to the traumas of my mind;
A place where I can hide and heal, that's never hard to find.
The antidote to what is past and thus what lies ahead:
I've found it in the comfort and the safety of my bed.

A never-changing presence in the middle of my room,
Which in some years became more like a closet or a tomb;
Enveloping, encasing me from daily stress and strain,
Where I could go to block away all memories and pain.
Away I'd flee from suffering, and overwhelming dread;
Applying to the comfort and the safety of my bed.

I've cried, and sobbed, and moaned, and wept, and ached, and mourned, and prayed,
And slept, and dreamed, and tossed, and turned, and battled when afraid;
My fears consuming night-times and my mornings as I'd waken,
As if the terrors swallowed me and I was left forsaken.
And yet, despite the struggles I endured within my head,
I'd wake within the comfort and the safety of my bed.

A place of nurture for such things as one's creative mind,
For words will come to me within the wellspring that I find;
A place to think, to write, to make, and, birthing something new,
I recognize my little universe deserves its due:
For this is where I've struggled, labored, toiled, worked, and bled:
A tribute to the comfort and the safety of my bed.

For it has not been such a haven solely just for me,
For it has been a respite also for my family;
I've hugged and cuddled, and wiped tears, and sung, read books, and prayed,
A mother's love, a grandma's love, both fervently conveyed.

Thus an extension of my heart, where open arms are spread:
Welcome to the comfort and the safety of my bed.

But in this bed I also knew what violation meant,
Enduring loveless love, in ways I tried to circumvent;
But now that time is past, so very far away from me,
That it remains the providence of fading memory.
So sanctified, restored, and dedicated now instead,
I triumph in the comfort and the safety of my bed.

Oh, wonderful and precious is this sacred place to me,
A temple where the psyche can abide, secure and free;
My inner world protected by an outer world of peace;
A mighty fortress where my cares, and woes, and fears decease.
For this is why the various enemies in life are fled:
My champion is the comfort and the safety of my bed.

In retrospect, and looking now, it does appear to me
Since that I've coped, it is the most exquisite therapy;
For this is how I've gotten through and managed to survive,
But not just that— I've done the more— by managing to thrive!
And so I lay here pondering what future lies ahead:
All glory to the comfort and the safety of my bed!

The Ability to Forget

Why should the past be brought again,
and resurrected from the dead,
engendering regret?
Why should we dredge up memories,
old specters of our miseries,
depleting all our energies,
rather than just forget?

What good is it to think again
of all that's past and gone before,
producing such upset
that fading wounds are never healed?
The scab that's picked will bleed, unsealed,
and trickle what was once congealed:
shouldn't we just forget?

The mind is very helpful, for it
has a proven, simple way
to rally from a threat:
it hides the hurt, makes wrong okay,
diminishing it day by day,
within a mental hideaway,
creating how we forget!

Considering the benefit
of such a mechanism, why
is there an issue yet?
Instead of letting traumas die,
remembering will amplify
the record. So, why not deny
those thoughts, and thus forget?

Here, I propose a remedy,
a healthy way to move ahead,
before what's done is set:

reliable for every need,
in outcome, it can be agreed,
this panacea's guaranteed:
the ability to forget!

To Be, or Not to Be Medicated

To burst unfettered in the manic way,
The talking mouth that cannot stop to rest,
Are you to say I should not be this way,
My fast brain bursting full of better, best?

I sing, I write, I make—but can these be
If creativity is dulled inside of me?
If sentience devolves to reticence,
To fit the current *psychopharma* sense,
How can I make the songs I sing so deeply
Or make the heart that hears it cry so sweetly?

I burn with heat as my pen works the page.
How can a dullard bring the sage words of a sage?
If neurons fire, then why misfire mine?
My flame will burn right out, without a rhyme!

You seek to keep the highs and lows at bay.
You wish to even out the peaks and pits:
But how can trees wave branches in the air
If they become attenuated bits?

My burst is lost! I love to burst!
I love to bear a child in a poem!

I love to work twelve hours at a thrust
To give in words a newly-labored tome!
I love to touch! I love to feel!
I love the sounds and hues of silk and steel!
If diamonds and rust escape the censoree,
Why do you seek to take it all from me?

"Ah yes, but see, you are complex:
Your mind is broke and needs a kind of fix.
We cannot have you run abouting–
Living, breathing, singing, shouting–
And thinking toomuchtoomuch, too–
So this is why these meds are good for you!"

Ah yes, I know!
The points on a momentary snowflake sparkle so!
And yet, if you were to smooth it smoothingly,
What shape would then the perfect snowflake be?

In fairness, I do go low to the abyss.
This pit is not when twirling my skirts
But rather when I'd render splits
Into my skin until it hurts.

I can make tombs of closets or my bed.
For sleeping hard and long can make you dead.

(But to a point) because I wake again.
'Tis true this ebb can flow out in the end.

Ah, to straddle polar poles and not to sway!

Healers of neuron makers and transmitters,
Give me back my brain's peculiar fritters!
Pharma, grant no side-affected me,
And Psyche will dance in manic revelry!

You are my better brain
for my mother, Ahni

When I am brimming over with life's
daily stress and strain,
you help me navigate the waves:
you are my better brain.

When I am blind, you help me see,
you help me ascertain
where I lack understanding, for
you are my better brain.

There have been times of chaos, when
I'd nearly gone insane,
but then your wisdom settled me:
you are my better brain.

You help me think: so numerous are
the thoughts I can't contain;
you help me hone a strong, lean mind:
you are my better brain.

You listen and you counsel, ears
that comfort and explain

in such exquisite therapy:

you are my better brain.

Through all the years of sorrow, wracked

with untold weights of pain,

you shared the load, and bore it, too:

you are my better brain.

Your powers of logic triumph,

for with reason you remain

victorious over my fallacies:

you are my better brain.

Your sage advice enlightens me,

obscurity made plain

by words, and thoughts, and facts, and heart:

you are my better brain.

And so I thank you: I am full,

recipient of great gain;

and if I'm richer it's because

you are my better brain.

I'm better now

I'm better now, though I was ill
for many years. Raw memories still
pervade my mind, for I can see,
dictated by insanity,
a fight for every force of will.

Pure manic energy, the thrill,
harsh dangers, foolish acts, until
judgment was gone; but thankfully
I'm better now.

Dark lowness that could bleed and kill,
hard emptiness, death, cold, and chill,
enchained; but now a change in me:
both poles subdued! Miraculously,
due to new pills, (and medical skill),
I'm better now.

PANTHEON

The Sonnet of JonBenet (1990-1996)

Six-year-old JonBenet Ramsey was found dead in the basement of her Boulder, Colorado home on Christmas morning, 1996.

A little girl was killed one winter day,
Her breath was taken from her. Someone hurt
This child and made a game or perverse play
In which her very body was to flirt
With danger and with pain. And so she died,
When for the love of pleasure or of power
Someone lay her down and used her as she cried.
Indeed, the strength of Hell sought to devour
This child, and used the ones perhaps who bare
Her— evil, twice-dead, rotten souls who fed
Upon this innocence, void of love or care.
Sweet Gilded Lily, painted, prodded, dead!

Oh child, will there ever be a way
When justice in your case will have its day?

The Trial of Saint Joan of Arc
(Burned at the stake, Rouen, Normandy, 30 May 1431)

You had to act, because you heard the voices
Within your head. Saint Michael came to you,
Saints Catherine and Margaret. But what choices
Did you have? You knew them to be true,
Not demons or deceit or rank delusion,
But speaking straight from God Himself. How bold
You were to listen and to act. Conviction
Had led you to an ultimate conclusion
Of capture, trial, suffering untold
As you were burned in perverse benediction.

How strange a concept that someone can die
So horrible a death for just belief
Or courage of conviction. You did try
To fight the inquiry without aid or relief,
The men who could not bear a different way
Of thinking or of acting. "*You're deceived!
Demonic! Under Satan! An apostate!
You have led the very world astray!*"
All because you acted and believed,
You then became the object of such hate!

In retrospect it seems it was a crime
To be a woman, different and strong,
Living well beyond the norms of time,
Defying convention as you went along.
How threatening to patriarchal power
Was one young, teenage female. Can it be
That just because you fought with all your might
The whole counsel of men sought to devour
And destroy you? You could not be free
To live; who was the one that was not right?

So many men against one little foe!
Almost still a girl! But not so much
In influence and power. And although
You were unusual, your life would touch
Your countrymen and women, who would see
In you a budding saint, who saw and heard
The world of angels, seeking yet the voice
Of God above all others. Fervently
You tried to be obedient to His word
As you did know it, for this was your choice.

"If I am not in grace, God place me there,"
You spoke of the salvation of your soul.
*"And if I am in grace, pray, keep me where
I am with Him."* You jostled up the whole
Of argument and all theology
Because you spoke the simple truth. Confound
The wise in all their own conceits! And when
You stumped them, speaking wisdom forcefully,
Enough for them to ponder all around:
A teenage girl against a horde of men.

But sadly, because you would not heed or bend,
You broke the rules until it was too late;
You then were relegated to your end:
A stake and fire, this would be your fate.
By burning bodies somehow sin will cease?
Somehow it stops the greater fires of hell?
A force-based, threatening theology,
And not free will, will never, ever cease
To stop conviction, as we see too well,
When voices thus combine with zealotry.

But in the end, you were not relegated
Among the damned and reprobate. We see
How now you have been wholly vindicated
By changing tides and course of history.
At first exonerated of all crime,
Then by a change of thought was glorified,

The judge's folly thus was realized.
Made martyress by passing of the time,
And then by certain rite beatified,
Then ultimately you were canonized.

What can we glean from you, in looking back?
Can we be glad for freedom of the will
Which we do have today? Do we still lack
A greater liberty? Is thinking still
Repressed and persecuted? Can there be
No room for differences or points of view?
Are there still inquisitions? Do we spurn
What we don't understand? Or do we see
That we can all be wrong, or not all true?
Or is this something we can never learn?

For Demetra, "of the fruitful soil."

Bearer of mental offerings
in lieu of formulae,
in lace your animus dwells:
pastels and purpose,
baby's breath and the scholar's sigh;
your roses root in figurings,
your reverie swells with harvest

We, golden stalks, like autumn wheat
are two strands amid a sea of hair;
yet root and trunk so closely lie
that when the wind wafts our seeded shafts
we bend in synchrony

Perhaps, when our Planter undertook
to till and hoe about us,
could He not have from one sapling
sliced a part away
to form us both?

Quasimodo

"Look not on the face, young girl, look at the heart."
— Quasimodo, The Hunchback of Notre Dame

A vile, lumbering mass, so hideous,
Rejected and despised by every eye
That fears and is repulsed by odious
Perversions of our kind. You horrify
And shock the average sensibility
For which all imperfection is rejected
And avoided. You are ugliness,
A limping lump of flesh. How you are affected
By the body of your wretchedness!

But souls, come look beyond the skin
And see a difference from within the heart!
Quasimodo, you are kind within
Your stricken, broken body. Counterpart
To your condition is this rarity
Of spirit and mind. Embodiment of good,
Self-sacrifice, compassion— for the love
That gives all from a place of charity
In spite of every pain is understood
To form within as well as from above.

It only took a single, cooling cup
Of water, but you drank with thankfulness;
And as La Esmeralda lifted up
Your sorry head, you looked with gratefulness
To one who chose a good deed on the day.
Oh, how this changed your lonely, saddened state
To gratitude and love from emptiness—
For now you loved her. Banished and away
All forms of mockery— a better fate
Because your form was touched by loveliness.

And then what? In her time of utmost need
You aided her. You rescued her, you saved
Her, sheltered her, protected her. Indeed
You gave back hundredfold for what she braved
In giving you that drink. But all in vain;
The gallows waited for her neck. You tried
To keep her from her date with hungry death
But all for naught. For you could not obtain
Her liberty. You watched her as she died,
And let a howl out with woeful breath.

You cried and no one heard your bitter groans,
But 'round your love were found your noble bones!

Blessed Margaret Plantagenet Pole (1472-1541)

Executed by Henry VIII, Tower of London, 27 May 1541

You ran around the room. The hooded goon
Was chasing with his ax. In tears and cries
You asked him "Why? What have I done?" But soon
He reached your aged neck. But nothing dies
Unless you kill it. Firmly, blood began
To spew from wound, and wound, and wound, and more
Than thirteen whacks and chops and strikes; a man
Against a woman. Then the hacking gore
Took off your head. The deed was done. Such strain
Of royal blood was by a Tudor shed,
Plantagenet and threatening and slain!
Made martyress by him who made you dead.

A coward and a tyrant, in the name
Of bullied blood beatified the same.

Martyress Anne Askew (1521- 16 July 1546)
Tortured and burned at the stake under the order of Henry VIII

They pulled your tortured body hard and long,
Click by wretched click the ropes distorting bent your frame;
Up they pulled, and down they pulled, along
The sinews ripping, muscles giving way, the tear, then came
The cracking and the breaking at the joints.
They knew the point of no return was there and passed when they
Applied the torque to snap connecting points
Of tendon, bone and movement. Hours then became the day
When you would never walk again. For torn
Apart you were and did remain; a wretched; racked apart;
Stretched and broken. To dying you were borne
Upon a chair to waiting fires; but not until your heart
Was burning did you cry out~ once for all
The pain, the terror, terrorizing, helplessness: the pain
Beyond all pain. Stretched ruins thus recall
The ruin of your body and the flames for unseen gain.

And herein is the greater mystery:
What gain? What benefit can come of being pulled apart?
Why suffer? Why deny the remedy?
Recalcitrant and stubborn! Give the words and leave your heart!
Surely you can please and can appease?
Nothing is this vital! Nothing matters more than life!
This is derangement! not to seek to ease
The torments of your body, all the wastings and the strife
Of life to forfeit~ wasted on belief!
What possibly compels someone to suffer willingly?
How could you enter on without relief
In light of forgone torture and a death in agony?

Aye, there's the rub: for not of what is seen
Is such a soldier made; this sterner stuff forms from a heart
Which sees and seeks a world beyond~ unseen,

Eternal, spiritual, angel habitation, set apart
For those who seek it and who hear the call
From there to here. A call to arms, the trumpet call, a cry,
To fight with courage, and to forfeit all
That seems important here and now. For such you chose to die.

For there are kings, and then a King indeed:
A loving King, a sovereign Lord who rules by different might,
Not of forced coercion but of need
Within the human heart for help and freedom from the plight
Of evil and of wickedness and sin;
This Lord became more than a Lord, because He came to be
Among us, like one of us, and within
The human heart He comes again to dwell and make it free.

And this you knew, that once for all He gave
His dripping blood, for He was stretched like you, His tender limbs
And sockets out of joint. That blood will save
The heart that calls upon Him, so powerful it dims
The bogus light of darkness. Bleeding light,
Red truth, bled goodness, loving blood! Oh, not of wine or bread
But what He did by bleeding makes us right
With Him. You could not say that wafers and then wine instead
Will save a willing soul; for this you died.
The racking failed and fires to reverse your fervent mind,
Because you knew that Once was crucified
Was once enough; the Book told you and you believed in kind.

And so your blood was burnt, as His was bled,
Your conscience not permitting otherwise. Posterity
Has seen your death and heard the words you said,
Not bending to the pressure to be easy or be free.

You taught us in convictions to be brave;
Not to give in to pressure in expediency, or fear
To choose a painful dying, or the grave.
Sweet mercy and no compromise is mercy most severe.

The Earl of Oxenford's Sonnet
(To Edward de Vere, 1550-1604)

Shakespeare! For so long I knew the image,
But not your person; for you have been kept
Obscured and obfuscated through the visage
Of ancient lies. Oh, how my whole heart leapt
When I through others' toils found your name!
It is de Vere, and Oxford, Edward; Earl
Of erudition, finest wit, the same
As the Spear-Shaker; our worded pearl,
But not the Poet-Ape. Your glory had
Too long been laid upon the upstart crow,
This man of nothing— fronting, homely, sad
Excuse for all you are and all you know.

For truth is truth, and you do shake a spear;
The Bard, the Age's Soul, divine de Vere!

Sebastian

An ode to Johann Sebastian Bach (1685-1750)
Sebastian: from Greek "venerable"

I touch the pages of your music. Then
My thoughts transport to times and distant sounds
Where you once dwelt. I think of you and when
I do a flood comes up from me, abounds
An all-consuming longing, yearning, ache.
Somehow I seem to feel what you once felt
When I begin to play or listen. Joy
Combined with sorrow, something you did make
An art form, from the losses you were dealt,
And morphing into beauty. You employ

All techniques of the mind and ear and heart
And reach my own. And I respond in kind,
And want to create beauty, too. A part
Of me belongs to you, because I find
You draw me into truth, and there I stay.
In reciprocity I always aim
To offer back to you, and God, the best
That I can offer when I sing. Today
I offer up an ode of love, and frame
It by the words I write. For I am blessed,

So truly blessed, to know the forms
In which you wrote. To sing chorales, cantatas!
A motet, mass or aria transforms
The mundane to sublime! A suite, toccatas!
A prelude, fugue, the passion of the Passions!
Magnificent Magnificat! Baroque
Complexity excites me to the core!
Concertos, and the Goldberg Variations!
The pain and truthful beauty! Come, evoke
The substance thus within me, this and more!

Your mastery of harmony, combining
Such frank, sweet melodies which touch the soul
With perfect counterpoint: thus intertwining
Of several, making many parts a whole.
For you know joy; exhilaration forms
The "happy Bach" who dances. Trumpets call
And organ-powers attest. But one can hear
The pains of loss and longing, for the storms
Of death did take ten children. We hear all;
In plaintive strings your sufferings appear.

Not only what is written on the pages
But what is at the top-- for there you write
Initials, signifying for the ages
Jesu, Juva, *"Jesus, aid."* And right
Below, the ending written, "S.D.G.",
For *Soli Deo Gloria*: alone
To God be glory. Prayer in music cast, when
Your heart is on display for all to see.
And so I feel a part of you my own;
A touch of soul-mate, friend, the great Sebastian.

The Wise Woman
to Carla Christopher

Priestess warrior of words and guardian of the souls who write,
You reach a mother's arm around to take the poet in,
And there inside that shelter place is surety of insight
Which aids each to discover and express her words within.

Because you open doors that for too many shut away,
I come to see here what I am and then what I am not;
And am thus less reluctant or afraid to stand and say
What I must say the way I say it, and thus when I cannot.

The priestess is also a warrior, for she fights for fights of rights
Of voiceless, meek, shy souls, afraid to take a word to page,
Or ones unsure of even who they are: your haven lights
A way of safety, which leads them to their pages, and then the stage.

In strength you are, wise warrior, wise woman, wise to face,
And are the poet mother whereby the artist finds her place.

Maxwell Schollenberger

Twelve-year old Maxwell Schollenberger was found dead in a home in Annville, Pennsylvania, in May 2020, where he had been starved, imprisoned in a dark room, and beaten for years.

A child was deprived of everything;
He spent his life in darkness, all alone;
Without the love that from a heart should spring—
But he had none; a normal life unknown.

They found his body lying on the bed,
Covered in excrement, no clothes to wear;
He was not sheltered lovingly, nor fed,
And not a soul to give him any care.

The room was dark, the windows boarded up,
And not the semblance of a shaft of light;
The only drink, a dirty plastic cup—
A bit of water, and no food in sight.

For he was so deprived, his body weighed
A fraction of what it was meant to be;
His muscles never moved, he never played:
How great the state of his infirmity!

This was not but a day, but it was years
That he was held, a prisoner of Hell;
And no one cared to wipe away his tears:
The very air possessed a putrid smell,

And there he lived, if you could call it life.
Day after day, year after wretched year,
Alone in stinking darkness, a state rife
With such abominations and such fear—

For he would cry and scream if someone came;
He knew the source of all his hurt and pain.

These demons from the molten pit became
His torturers, and there he would remain

In living, dying Hell! Oh, precious boy!
You never got to live, to run and play!
You never even had a simple toy
Or got to see the brightness of the day!

And as I think, what most surprises me
Is that for twelve long years he lived somehow;
He lay in dark and filth, in misery!
Oh, how I wish that he were cared for now!

For he was starved and beaten on the day,
And he was at the end killed by a blow,
Combined with body weakness, passed away:
The only human contact he would know.

At least it seems that justice will prevail,
And these two monsters that imprisoned him
Are now in turn imprisoned in a jail,
Where I do hope their punishment is grim!

Oh, dear, sweet boy, I do expect you know
The joy of love now; with the angels bright
You are abiding, where young children go,
And such past wrongs in Heaven are made right!

Goodbye, Sweet Fetal Child

Goodbye, sweet fetal child— for you shall die,
Because a mother's love is also dead:
The hallowed place of nurture where you lie
Shall soon become the ground where blood is shed.
The battle to reject the womanly,
Or motherly, for "me, myself and I"
Shall forfeit noble care of progeny
(That greater good): hence hearts have gone awry.
The battlefield where "what is hers" to keep
Claims hedonistic "choice" its weaponry;
But poison, scalpel, pill or force will reap
That bitter fruit, bare yet the casualty.

For those untimely born, it must suffice
That they, not choice, become the sacrifice.

The Ballad of Babi Yar

Over 100,00 people were killed at Babi Yar between September 29, 1941 and November 6, 1943.

Oh, come and gather round to hear
This story from afar,
As I unfold the tragedy,
The tale of Babi Yar.

It happened in the time of war,
And not to be outdone,
Aggression reared its ugly head
In 1941.

For Germans drove the Russians out
Of Kiev in Ukraine;
And there they set up their command:
Ruthless and inhumane.

For after Russian bombings of
The city, vengeance grew;
The Germans found their answer~ this
Was what they chose to do:

"The Yids, they are responsible!
Those Jewish Bolsheviks!
We know we must retaliate
Against their cunning tricks!"

For there, outside the city, was
This natural ravine,
Which then became a killing field,
Macabre, a nightmare scene.

"All Yids in Kiev must report,
And if you don't, you will
Be shot; make sure you do as told
Or else we're sure to kill."

And so, naively, all Jews came
And waited on the day
Unknowingly, to meet their end
As they were hauled away.

*"Strip off your clothes, and put your things,
Your valuables in a pile,
And line up here- do as you're told,
And wait a little while."*

Then one by one, they, line by line
Approached the precipice;
And naked told to face it
While they gazed at ghastliness.

For every row of Jews was shot
And face down they did fall
Into the ever-growing pile
Of bodies. One and all,

Well over thirty thousand souls
Would perish in two days,
Machine guns filling the ravine.
And when their bloody ways,

Their bloodlust wasn't satisfied,
They came for the insane-
The hospital was emptied. Plus
The gypsies from Ukraine,

As well as Russian soldiers captured,
Kiev citizens,
Communists and ordinary
Soviet denizens.

Nude bodies struck, the women raped,
They buried the half-dead;
Or stepping on the bleeding pile
Would shoot to kill instead.

The little children, babies, were then
Hurled into the air,
Over the edge, into the pit,
Before their mothers there.

And then, they tried to shield their crime
In 1943,
By disinterring every corpse,
And in some secrecy

Would burn away the evidence.
And so for forty days
A hundred thousand dead or more
Became as ashen haze.

But this was all in vain because
In time the world would know
What happened in that deep ravine
Those many years ago.

For it indeed behooves us that we
Learn from this, and then
No more repeat the ugly past,
No never, not again.

And so, memorials today
Remind us, insofar
As we maintain the memory of
The dead of Babi Yar.

MUSIC'S MADE THROUGH IT

If I could access

If I could access musicality
And thus create a different kind of art
(Such writing as should set a work apart),
I then would have the perfect poetry.

If I could use the gift of melody
To make my writing intone from the heart,
And I could create rhythm, counterpart
To blending words in verbal harmony,

Then I would have a work that truly sings,
With song-like quality, and with a voice
With which I could be happy, and rejoice
That poems can rise above mere common things.

For I'd be satisfied: my mind-heart girds
My writing to make music from my words.

My Piano

Because this rarity was given me,
Among musicians I am truly blessed;
I touch refined and black mahogany:
This instrument is better than the rest.
In tonal quality it is the best,
So pure in clarity that it is near
Perfection. I appreciate this, lest
I am not grateful. Easily you hear
The sweetness and vibrations that are clear
And resonant. The keys are to the feel
Responsive and receptive; to the ear
A satisfaction; beauty in ideal.

Miraculous in all its aural ways,
My Steinway's panegyric: laud and praise!

Oh, when I hear

Oh, when I hear the plaintive, painful sound
Of music played within a minor key,
Or modal scales in doleful reverie,
Suspensions and its dissonance abound.
A juxtaposing light and dark around
A center of discordant harmony
Combined with the most weeping melody
Is where a truth, so sacred, may be found.
For it is in the ebbing resolution,
When tensions ease and struggling is at rest,
That one can find a consonant conclusion,
And peace from pain residing in the breast.
For suffering can be of benefit,
If acquiescing, music's made through it.

Steinway Pantoum

How can I love an object like I do?
It's almost like I have a lover's heart
and I'm in love. But do not misconstrue,
somehow it works in sync, in counterpart!

It's almost like I have a lover's heart:
I wish to make love as I touch the keys
somehow; it works~ in sync, in counterpart,
and like two lovers, who will give and please.

I wish to make love; as I touch the keys
I play, and somehow it responds in kind;
and like two lovers, who will give and please~
its tone the sweetest gifting to my mind.

I play, and somehow it responds in kind
and offers up a most unearthly sound:
its tone the sweetest gifting. To my mind,
responsiveness in action rarely found,

and offers up a most unearthly sound.
The lover and beloved combined as one;
responsiveness in action rarely found,
to touch perfection, not to be outdone.

The lover and beloved, combined as one,
and I'm in love! But do not misconstrue.
To touch perfection, not to be outdone:
how can I love an object like I do?

The Sacred Harp

"Seek the old paths and walk therein."– B.F. White

The music, oh the music starts, and we
Begin to sing in skillful harmony;
Begin to sing in sweet simplicity;
Begin to sing in deep complexity.

The stirring of the beat enlivens me:
My soul awakes in singing earnestly;
Of many, one, in practice poignantly;
To sing in sacred musicality.

We use a musical democracy,
Where each in turn in expressivity,
For each to get a chance the lead to be:
The square is individuality.

Within the hollow square is mystery:
God choosing to reveal Himself to me.

The Neglected Piano

As if it has a speaking voice
I hear it beckoning,
Calling, calling, calling in a
hush of whispering.

"Oh, come, and do not pass me by,"
I seem to hear it say.
*"Do not ignore my silent plea:
Come, and sit, and play!"*

For when I seem to overlook
Its honest ebony
I turn and see the waiting keys,
In pearled ivory.

They yearn to have my touch and then
I yearn to touch them, too,
And stop procrastinating
With this thing and that to do.

"I cannot make my music,"
(Gives its gentle reprimands)
*"It's all potentiality
Except for both your hands.*

*For all the works that you adore
Are locked inside of me,
Unless you come and open them:
Your fingers are the key.*

*The Chopin that you love so much
Is waiting patiently,
Or all your Bach chorales, and hymns
Are urging silently!"*

And then I realize that I
Am blessed beyond all measure
With this fine, Steinway instrument;
This pleasure is a treasure.

And so I sit and touch the keys,
And it responds in kind,
In thankfulness with beauteous tones
That touch both heart and mind.

Lest I ignore its whispered call
I'll, each and every day,
Thus satisfy the patient keys
And not neglect to play.

The Classical Singer's Drink Offering

"In the holy place shalt thou pour out a drink-offering of strong drink unto the LORD" –Numbers 28:7

I reach my fingers to the fret or key,
And heave a deeper sigh than heretofore;
I hum, and buzz, and palpitate— the spree
Of writhing soul and senses in my store.

I charge exactitude from vocal strings,
And from the plucked ones gentle company;
I spill and turn my gut with inner things
That seeks to spew them out in melody.

I move my inner body to the beat.
I die, and die, and pour out juice afresh:
With each new grasp or howl, moan or bleat
My body vibrates now. The shaking flesh

Holds sturdy little chords that touch in kind.
Oh truthful tone! Like off a church's vaulting, waft
In echoes of purity. Not merely mind But sorrow makes this music, bitter craft
Which carves in order to expand, and stabs
That wounds may bleed out color, depth and hue.
(A voice without these contributions grabs
At self-inspired purpose, aiming not to
Glorify the art or Artisan.)

But after the heaves and pants, the shimmer, the ring,
The chill-bumps in the hairshafts, when my blood
Has leapt and circled corpuscular gamuts, filling
My mask with heat and sound, a kind of thud
Percusses my environs. I turn around
As if to see Him watching.

Oh, to face
Not loving half so much my very sound,
As Him for whom this pouring out took place.

THE EBBS AND FLOWS OF LIFE

If I knew then

If I knew then what I know now,
if I had had a godly sorrow,
if I had hindsight of many years,
if I had yielded not to fears,
then I would have some good to show.

Then my soil would not be fallow;
and fruitful harvestings would grow,
and I would not have shed such tears,
if I knew then.

For I would go back and say "no"
to sins and choices from below
and action from my yesteryears
to which my present life adheres,
with damages and fates of woe,
if I knew then.

Twisted Reckoning

If pain can produce beauty,
and if beauty causes pain,
then how can I be reconciled
to more loss than I gain?

If love is also longing,
and if love is loss refined,
how can I move ahead and mourn
when love has been unkind?

I look afar aback on life,
I see in retrospect
how vain were my attempts to love
what love came to reject.

I furtively sought on and on
to find camaraderie,
but come to this: I am alone
with I, myself and me.

But loneliness can transmorph pain
and become one at last;
I breathe in states of solitude
like penance due my past.

I learn of quiet and unrest,
in paradox I stay;
and thus endeavor to find out
why life has been this way.

And so I edge along ahead
with one big questioning:
why have I lost what others gain,
this twisted reckoning???

Have I forgotten? ❧

Have I forgotten all these years before,
when life was such a struggle every day?
Don't I recall these hard times anymore,
when it was difficult to find my way?

When life was such a struggle every day,
I worked and strived and labored arduously;
when it was difficult to find my way,
relief seemed very far away from me.

I worked and strived and labored arduously.
In trying to survive and then achieve,
relief seemed very far away from me,
endeavoring each day without reprieve!

In trying to survive, and then endure,
don't I recall these hard times anymore?
Endeavoring each day without reprieve~
have I forgotten all these years before?

From this tortured bond

From this tortured bond release me,
Do not, sovereign Lord, disdain:
For if health and freedom please thee,
Bring the antidote to pain!

For my weakened body fails me:
Always hurting, little rest;
Head and throbbing limbs ache sorely;
Twisted spinal nerves compressed;

Let alone the sacred places
Where the soul must cry alone;
Eyes and tears and voice leave traces
Wherein spirit can only moan!

Shall the dark night wane with dawning?
Do you wish me to depart?
Have you finished with me early?
Have you finished with my heart?

For time is not a friend of worth:
It ages body and soul;
Were I to join you from this earth
I'd then be fully whole.

But should you wish a warrior
To continue in this fight,
Then would you be my Champion and
Defend me with your might?

For I am failing in my woe,
I've not the strength to be;
One of us will have to go:
Either him, or me.

These Thirty Years

These thirty years of love and woe,
Of motherhood, when I did sow
The seeds of lives, for me to keep
And nurture, until they would reap
The fruits of what they'd have to show:

From womb, to breast, where prayers did flow
As they grew up, so they could know
A good life, how my heart did weep
These thirty years.

Yet they have blossomed all, although
Their challenges were hard, and so
They rose above, a quantum leap
Beyond their peers, both high and deep:
Success and my tears overflow
These thirty years.

The Homeless Sonnet

I have no shelter from the bitter storm.
I have no refuge or a hiding place.
I have no sanctuary, solid, warm,
Secure or safe; no respite, rest, or solace.

In endless fruitless journeys I uproot
What little hold I make, only to mourn,
And transplant all my withered, sickened fruit
Again to other soil, tired and worn.

How great the evil in me! Or the sin,
That this perpetual harvest, reaped and sown,
This endless nothing, this bitter Wheel, will win
The fight; I cannot live to fight alone.

A fireplace; wood floors; wallpaper; earth;
A settled bed; my children's future; mirth.

To a dead friendship

How many years we've known each other's lives,
And kept in touch with intermittent care:
From childhood's dreams to hope where hope survives—
We've seen each other grow from here to there.

And like a sailing ship whose journey sends
It drifting far away to distant lands,
Our certain courses, once as friends to friends
Have parted ways, as destiny demands.

But dear one, please do not attempt to force
Against the winds or tides that God made be:
Directions change, and with it our course
Of life; let ours remain in memory.

For though within my heart I love you so,
I also love enough to let you go.

An Adoptee's Reflection

I've never felt that I was like the rest,
Because I did not have what others do—
A normal blood family, for most are blessed
With knowing mother, father, kindred, too.
I grew up always wondering about
The person that I really was — who were
These parents of biology? I doubt
I ever rested; how my thoughts would stir!
And then I found my mother years ago,
An English and Germanic combination;
But now I've found my Jewish father— know
How full of wonder, this new revelation!

For all those things I yearned for deep inside
At last have come to me; I'm gratified.

What's in a name?

What's in a name? What does it mean
to have identity?
I had a name, but was unseen,
for it was false to me.

I could not live a lie, and so
I'm now who I must be,
I've shed the pretense— for I now know:
the truth has set me free.

For falsehood is not true to me,
and so I took the name
of my true blood and family,
the blood from which I came.

For knowledge is a powerful force,
and now what's been revealed
is who I was, and am— the source
by which my name's been sealed.

No need to wonder anymore,
for science did bestow
the answer I've been searching for:
who am I? Now I know.

Guard your heart

Guard your heart: for sacred is its space,
And few deserve its access or its view,
Or fewer still its treasures, hidden, too,
Protected by its covert dwelling place.
Do not allow just anybody in,
For desecration follows such an act;
Destruction and defilement within
Will follow when so heinously attacked.

For there are only those who prove their worth
By loving as you love, and also care
As you do, in sadness and in mirth,
When both upon one's fate are brought to bear.
For nothing shows contempt like apathy,
Poison devoid of reciprocity.

I am alone

I am alone, though I have tried
to offer what has been denied,
to love both friends and lovers, yet
rejection partners with regret
to fashion how I now abide.

The open rawness cries inside,
yet I am always mystified,
perplexed at how my fate is set;
I am alone.

I take this kismet in my stride,
(due diligence has been applied),
but wonder nags at what I get:
Why do my efforts thus beget
the many tears that life has dried?
I am alone.

The fallen vestige

The fallen vestige of her foliate time:
Browned leaves beneath; coarse needles of old pine
Once green and pungent; when her nests in spring
With peeping chicks, and swaying boughs, would sing.

So splendors fade, as does the daily light;
Of seed and growth and birth and bloom and height:
Such pastels surely rise to later blend
Into the morose darks of autumn end.

But when to earth her fullness drops like tears,
It thus becomes the soil of future years.

THE CHANGE THAT COMES WITH AGE

The Rise of Fall

There were such pretty flowers in the spring:
The fragrant colors of a verdant time;
Such fresh potentiality, sublime
In all the loveliness that they did bring.
Then summer issued forth a deep wellspring,
Maturely ripening, where vines would climb
And trees begin to bulge. This is the prime
Of life when growth will dance and sway and sing.

But autumn is the time of now. I stand
Amid the harvests and the fruit. The change
Between the then and now, it leaves me jaded;
I barely have the bearings to withstand
This person of today. Indeed, how strange,
How much the beauty of the past has faded.

I once was sharp as blades

I once was sharp as blades, as honed as steel,
and I could slice raw words within my mind
and then put them to paper, thus consigned
to publish all I think, believe and feel.
I was as bright as day, and was as real
as sunlight which can make the viewer blind:
so sharp and light did become intertwined,
and beauties from within to all reveal.

But now I am as dull as rotten wool;
my thoughts are nothing if not addlepated;
my acumen seems gone into a pile
of sweet, soft nothing. Once so strong and full
of clarity, but now deteriorated,
I wonder how my efforts are worthwhile.

Last Evening's Glance

As I glanced into the mirror, what I saw
Surprised my eyes. Oh, who is this I see?
What do I see? This visage leaves me raw!

Is this reflection what is truly me?
Or is it some perverse, sick apparition?
What happened to the me I used to be?

Oh, am I really in this sad condition?
Are all these changes really real and true?
Or am I seeing just a rank distortion?

Come, look at all the defects I can view!
The only thing remaining are my eyes,
Which do not change as other features do.

I look about my face and realize
The ghost of what I used to be is there
But its full form will not materialize!

I cross-examine all my face with care;
Instead it is a phantom of the past,
No former forms of glory anywhere!

And yet, the eyes do have it, for they cast
From deep within a certain shining light,
Retaining all the beauty of the past.

And it is there where you can glean a sight
Of our true nature, who we are— and now
Revealing spirit, will, and strength, and might

Of the whole person. For the eyes allow
A window to the soul. But it's my face
That perturbs me and disturbs me anyhow!

Despite the wizening, a certain grace
Remains amid the wrinkled, aging skin.
For life will leave its scars and marks, and trace

The everywheres and places we have been
Upon our brows and cheeks. It is not kind,
This revelation of our all within!

But somehow amidst all of this, I find
A consolation, that to me at least
This changed and changing face is not my mind!

And so, in some sense, I have been released
From all complaining, and my rant is ceased!

Self-Portrait

An aging, slowly fading entity;
A greying heart and changes of the mind;
The autumn time of life has come to me,
And I am quite surprised at what I find.

For I am still the same as I have been—
The ball of intense passion full inside;
The person that I am is still within,
Though sometimes I do feel that part has died.

For yes, I have the fire, but its flame
Is flickering and smoldering away;
In many ways it will not be the same
As when full fire forced its light on day.

For change of life's a curiosity,
For what I was, and am, and am to be.

What once was is no more

What once was is no more. I say goodbye
To youth and to the struggles of the past,
And sometimes shed a tear. I stand steadfast,
And look ahead, and then I heave and sigh,
And mourn the loss of what has come to die.
The unavoidable will thus contrast
With sprightly, lively living that has passed;
This new-old entity can mystify.

I now accept the change that comes with age:
The greying and the fading energies
That cause me to look inward, as a sage
Would, finding meaningful philosophies;
And still I put my thoughts and heart to page
In hopes that I retain my faculties.

What if my time

What if my time is limited? if all
That I have left is perhaps months, not years,
All laden with the worries and the fears
Surrounding what is death. Can I recall
A time when all the cares of life were small,
And I would not yield up to silent tears,
Or what to high anxiety adheres,
As I am just about to take a fall?

I need a calm and steady state of mind,
Where I can take control of the unknown,
The frightful darkness that can make me blind,
The secret terror place that is my own;
I must thus steady stay, and then remind
My weaker self what better thought has known.

Full Circle

The tiny fertile soul is open, waiting, hoping, and ready to bloom.
And it blooms into saplings of fervent green, petals raised like arms to the sky,
ready to hold and embrace.

And then as the expectancy of the warming sun causes petals and leaves to open,
the sapling is uprooted by the roots.

Quivering, it slinks back, because within is still
such hope that it regains its place within the earth and soil.

Only again for seeds to be plucked off and eaten before their time,
once the plant could bear any fruit at all.

Those seeds were sown by effluence indeed,
but not in a place of beauty of open ground,
but in the slime pit of garbage and detritus, rust and refuse.
They grow into a likeness coated with wretched grief and grime.

Whereas now the plant is fully matured, a tree beyond the age of seeds and fruit.
Alone and reaching upward still.
The leaves turn bright when they are ready to die,
before they fall away and down to make a place to trample underfoot again.

And when the branches bear no more,
and when the roots can take in no more water,
when all that is brittle dries and snaps and cracks
and even the birds do not make their nests any more in her,

perhaps then can she be acknowledged, dead but useful,
as her form, solid and strong,
can be sawed asunder, planed, hewn,

into purposeful things
for something other: person, time or place.

Perhaps the tree can be remembered,
if only for the grain and density,
which remains of her solid form.

Unless the earth prefers to return her into the soil she lived in once again,
where once grew the moans and squeals of winds and tweets of birds within her limbs.

And so her trunk is sliced near to the bottom, near the showing of the roots, and she falls hard against the earth,
her final sound.

The grey and knotted bark breaks off in pieces upon impact.
Naked is the pale, stripped wood against the hardened ground, for all to see if the trunk would be so moved.

The rest is still and silent.

EVER TOWARDS UNCERTAINTY

By My Conscience

I often find that it perplexes me
That I am neither to the left, nor right;
The battles fought of ideology
I do not have the wits within to fight.

For I am too conservative to be
A liberal in the ordinary sense,
And much too liberal for the GOP;
And so it seems I'm straddling the fence.

But I do have my causes and such things
As matter to my heart in all conviction:
When fuller, rounder views my viewing brings,
I cannot squeeze into a neat constriction.

So my identity is thus unknown;
But by my conscience it is clearly shown.

Oh, what is prayer?

Oh, what is prayer? Is it a mystery,
That bridges earth and heaven in a cry,
That reaches to the infinite? A sigh,
A groan, a whisper, tears that come to be
Admixed from faith and high anxiety
Or deep recesses of the soul. Whereby
The being arches up, and in, to try
To touch omnipotence with probity.

But sometimes silence follows all the din
Of many fears, and questions, and requests;
And sometimes there is nothing in return,
Or yet at least it seems this way. Within
The quake and hard unknowing rests
Desire yet: to seek, and burn, and yearn.

To want the things I want

To want the things I want: am I so wrong
When it is innocent activity?
To write a poem, or sing a hymn or song
And bring forth all the goings on in me?

Am I so wrong when I express my heart
Or when I offer mental ponderings?
Do these things keep my faith in God apart
And cause belief to wave in wonderings?

If God has given minds to think, then why
Is it all wrong to write down all my musing?
And is it wrong to open up and try
To share it all, no matter how confusing?

No matter what, I know Whom I've believed;
I only hope I haven't been deceived.

Where is the fire?

Where is the fire that once burned so bright?
Where is the eager faith that I once had?
Where is the happiness, where I was glad
To share my Lord and know him in his light?
I once had so much energy of heart,
And fervor, that my light would shine to all,
And confidence in the believer's call,
But now his grace and I are far apart.

It seems that all is dead and gone. No more
Do embers and the burning flames grow high
Or deep within me. Emptiness abounds,
And dryness. Oh, the Lord that I adore,
Or did adore— oh, are you far, or nigh?
My lack perplexes, saddens, and confounds.

The prayers of youth

The prayers of youth begin with fervent heat,
And all the passions of a lover's love,
And all the ardor of an earnest, sweet,
Excited faith, transcendent from above.

But as we age, our prayers, liked finest wine
Grow dry but complex. Nothing like before,
But staying steady on. Oh, where is mine,
The fires of my youth, oh, where the store

Of heat and passion, that seems now so dead?
It is more even now. Not without fire,
Just more an ember, which maintains instead
And makes a glow and warmth out of desire.

Oh, keep me on the warm and lighted way,
That you might fan me when I go astray.

The simple, stalwart faith

The simple, stalwart faith that I've aspired
To have is showing signs that I have erred;
Where once my very heart and soul were bared
Is now a place where prayers are uninspired.
This dross of what is left is undesired,
Worthless, empty, useless, when compared
To better times, when tears were unimpaired,
And all the zeal within my breast was fired.

Oh, what good is it now? Where is the light
That lit this darkened darkness? Now I strive
To say regurgitated prayers. I fight
To offer something earnest and alive.
It seems it all is gone. It is not right,
This present state. Will faithlessness survive?

Fool's Wisdom

"The fool has said in his heart, there is no God" Psalm 14:1
"I am fearfully and wonderfully made" Psalm 139:14

I am amazed at what some fools believe
Who say I am a fool to have belief
In a creative force. To preconceive
Against this possibility is chief
Among the many errors of our age.
For what takes faith? That life somehow began
As slime in a primordial soup? The sage
Would differ; wisdom clearly sees a plan,
Design, intent, and logic; every cell
Tells us the workings of a greater mind,
An artist to acknowledge seemly well
If we but ponder, look, and seek, and find.

Such handiwork abundantly displayed:
So fearfully, so wonderfully made.

A Sectarian Sonnet

"For ye are like unto whited sepulchers, which indeed appear beautiful outward, but are within full of dead men's bones, and of all uncleanness."
Matthew 23:27

How odd to me that in the agape feast
It is from Christians whom I feel this least:
With judging glances, or a waxen smile
Which bids to me, but only for a while
Until the meeting's over; then the same
Tight factions splinter smugly as they came:
Full of stale complaints, or all suspect
That each knows better than the other sect
Of this great thing or that; worse, to deride
And not embrace the social misfit's side.
And yet in amplitude and decibel
They praise a deafened god! or shout from hell.

The open, whitewashed sepulchers within
Are full of dead men's bones, uncleanness, sin.

The so-called heathen world

The so-called heathen world, the lost, the damned,
The non-confessing, creedless piles of humanity
Are sorted by degree of darkness, banned
By darker decree from light or health or sanity
Save by a formula. Wizardry makes potions,
Not antidotes. Imbibing (without credit
To the Alchemist) jolts clever notions
Of such evangelism, having read it
(The doctrine of some manual), that to drink,
One must first hear by man, and then repent.
But thirsty throats and morbid souls might think
To search the nameless Fluid being sent.

For every drop to mercy does allude;
And every heart is pagan, not imbued.

A Holy Offering

Of what I have, I lift up everything:
No less than all, no more than utterly;
My whole life is a holy offering.

I do not slice away a single thing,
But keep intact this inner treasury
Of what I have. I lift up everything,

For love, and pain, and hurt, and wounds which sting
Are all a part of spirituality,
My whole. Life is a holy offering:

It is not just the prayers or tears that spring
From faith, but also from the curiosity
Of what I've had. I lift up everything,

Admixing all together, worshipping
With body, soul and spirit earnestly—
My whole life. Hence, a holy offering:

The secular ascends as a wellspring,
And joins the sacred place where He shall be.
Of what I have, I lift up everything;
My whole life is a holy offering.

One of the Four Last Things

The Four Last Things, according to Christian eschatology, are Death, Judgment, Heaven, and Hell.

If I misunderstand the terms of what I have to face,
Then I perhaps misunderstand the meaning of your grace;
If hell awaits me still despite my many tears of shame,
Then what is hope? Then there is none: resulting is the same.

I weep in grief and guilt and fear, I weep for all my sin;
I weep because of what I've done without, and more, within;
I weep for pain I've caused, I weep for others' injury,
I weep still then for what others in sin have done to me.

And I could keep on weeping, fearing of the Judgement Day,
Because I fear still more that choosing you'll cast me away;
And in the hell of separation I will there remain
Without you, Lord: the reds and blacks of darkness and of pain!

Because my sins are such great sins, there is no remedy,
Except that you look down and choose to love and pity me;
I choose you and I follow you and still I follow more,
And yet I feel it's not enough and you will shut the door—

And then what door is there for me? What passage would there be?
How can I face you when I die and meet eternity?
O mercy, mercy, mercy Lord, upon my sinful soul,
I am so sorry for what wrongs my will would not control!

Unless you choose to choose me I can never follow you;
You must decide you want me so that I can want you, too;
Oh, pity, Lord! Oh, pity! May these salty bitter tears
Invoke salvation from your blood and stay my hell-fire fears!

For if you do not love me first, how can I then love you?
So Lord, I ask you: love me, so that I will love you, too;
I want a home in heaven and with you I want to dwell;
Oh, save me from the evil one, damnation and from hell!!!

The Salvation of my Soul

I do not wish to live in daily fear,
Afraid of what the future holds for me,
Afraid the time of reckoning is near
And I will meet God in eternity.
This worrying has taken its full toll;
I pray for the salvation of my soul.

What to believe? That everything is fine,
Because I was immersed, or on my head
Water applied? Salvation thus is mine?
Because of ritual I abandon dread?
Can I the virtues of this rite extoll?
I pray for the salvation of my soul.

Because, it is by faith, I've also heard,
And not an act performed in piety,
But by conversion of the heart. The Word
Says to believe: is this security?
Is Heaven's access in my full control?
I pray for the salvation of my soul.

For what if I should fall away, and leave
My God and faith? What saves me then? Oh, woe
Is me, for if it's up to me, I grieve,
Because there is no hope. But this I know:
To understand remains my present goal.
I pray for the salvation of my soul.

And so I am perplexed: it's not the will
Of man, or flesh, or animal blood that brings
About salvation: did Christ's blood fulfill
The law? I'm caught between disparate things.
I yearn to know the truth— not part, the whole:
I pray for the salvation of my soul.

The Supreme-Breasted One (*El Shaddai*)

El Shaddai has been interpreted by some to mean "the mountains of God" or "the God with breasts"

The woman in my Father's face,
The *ruach* of my soul;
Male images have hid the shad,
The breast, that *El Shaddai* has had
To comfort those, who wounded, have
Quite never been made whole.

Born anew? Yes; a birth it is—
But only from the pronoun "His"?
When earthly form so plainly shows
That woman is in what seed grows
And germinates, and procreates?
And she, whom Comfort has made flesh
To show His less, nay, more than "manliness":
That He is really also "She"—
A femininity in Trinity?

Oh yes! Oh blind paternals! Who do you think your Mother is?
Or has it never bothered you
That God could be a Mother, too?
(You may think this idea is new,
But male and female, in the image "His,"
Were long before theology, created.)
Is not our present view,
The image halved, unsolved, vastly untrue?

Can we deny our Author right
To words and views which may help light
This darkened, incompleted sight?
If God's eternal Word could flesh partake,
(A flesh of only woman, too) can we
Deny to let that Word be free
To partake fleshly female nouns? Did "He"

Establish this dichotomy?
We shall soon see.

Oh *Ruach*, blessed Spirit, in Hebrew tongue
The praise of Elohim is sung,
A masculine noun in text.
But yours, against device, is feminine!
Shekinah, God's glory; *Torah*, God's teaching; and next
Is *Chokhmah*, God's wisdom: all feminine, too.
Can we shun
What God has begun
Long before the Patriarchs hung
Their bias before our eyes? Can a Son
Have only one parent, the masculine?

"*But wait*," you may say, "*you're destroying the types. We know
That Christ will wed the Church; She
Is the very femininity
Of which you seek.*"
True; but it perplexes me
How male and female form His bride,
But with God's clearly female side
We choose to commit matricide.

The Spirit labors with child. Second birth, second womb;
Our self has died and left us vacancy
That Her First-Born may fill. Into the tomb,
Holy Seed, to quicken the human soul in urgency!

Now delivered, life from Life is come:
O feed me, fill me, Supreme-Breasted One.

Wrong

I've thought and practiced what I've known,
my faith's been fast and strong;
for all these years I've preached and prayed—
But what if I've been wrong?

I lived my core beliefs each day,
in poetry and song,
in music and the written word,
convinced I was not wrong!

I had conviction! I was right!
*"My world and I belong
to truth!"* But could it all be false?
What if my truth was wrong?

Oh, I was adamant, secure,
dogmatic, and headstrong,
because I knew! and you did not!
Could I have been this wrong?

How could it be that everything
I kept throughout lifelong
belief and practice falls away,
because I've found I'm wrong?

But isn't truth objective? far
beyond where all along
I said, *"I'm right! I know! You don't!"*
How then was I so wrong?

My current state's in flux, but
I would rather not prolong
the misery of uncertainty,
the state of being wrong!

So now, I've changed my point of view—
convictions fall headlong
into a pit of wondering:
What's truth? What's right? What's wrong?

I've said goodbye

I've said goodbye to Jesus, who
had been my guide and stay
(or so I thought); I'm now prepared
to go another way.

I've doubted, questioned, feared, and ached,
by working through inside
my heart's and mind's conundrums, where
reason and faith collide.

Too many unknowns, wonderings,
objections, arguments,
prognostications, prophecies,
warnings and portents.

No longer sure, because I've learned
too much to stay the same,
I can't go back, I can't stay still;
the facts assume the blame.

There is too much uncertainty,
too much of which to doubt,
and too much evil in his name,
which made me to want out.

And so I'm atheistic as to
his divinity,
and miracles, and words— he lived;
the rest's unsure to me.

Because my heart was rooted where
deception's power can hide,
I've had to look beyond this scope,
where conscience can abide.

Can I still love the God I love?
Can I go on from here?
Creator, God of Israel, rend
my heart from doubt and fear!

I still go on; my Jewish soul
discovered an old way,
the holiness of Mussar: learn,
renew, think, act, and pray.

Exodus 12

"And when I see the blood, I will pass over you." Exodus 12:13

As you have commanded, the blood to
The lintel and the doorposts of my heart
Has been applied. Because I've done this, through
Your power, sin and death are kept apart
From life. I am protected, singled out
From the destroyer seeking to destroy
My soul. Come, rid me of the fears and doubt
About eternity that rob my joy
Within this present state. I worry so
About the future, after all is said
And done, and I meet death. Instead, you know
I quake with apprehension and with dread.

Oh, take me where I can and will be free;
For when you see the blood, pass over me.

Baruch HaShem (Blessed Be the Name)

You are the God who once did write in stone,
And now upon the human heart you burn
Your holy words and ways, so we might yearn
To seek, and yield, and weep, and pray, and moan.
Oh, *Elohim*, and *Adonai*, alone
You are the Lord. You cause the soul to turn
And seek your face and will, that one may learn
Such truths and treasures heretofore unknown.

Oh, I am heavy laden in my breast,
That you, oh *El Shaddai*, great Breasted-One,
Are not embedded in me. With my whole
Being I desire to be blessed
As Jacob was, not letting go, till done.
In this I know I have a Jewish soul.

So many times

So many times I have been wrong before,
When I was certain that my way was right;
But now I'm not so certain anymore,
For wisdom earns its place within hindsight.

I used to think that what belonged to me,
And what I thought, and felt, and thus believed
Was truth, although I have begun to see
How oft I was egregiously deceived.

For rule, and ordinance, dogma, verity,
Practice, tenet, doctrine, sacrament,
Custom, credo, ideology
Immix into a morass of dissent.

The only truths seem as I age to be
Devolving ever towards uncertainty.

ACKNOWLEDGEMENTS

I would like to thank the following poetic colleagues: Hank Whittemore, Carla Christopher, James Sale, Andrew Benson Brown, James Tweedie, Evan Mantyk, Carol Smallwood, Joseph S. Salemi, Sally Cook, Margaret Coats, James B. Nicola, Hiram Larew, Patricia Asuncion, Larry Robin, Jane Stahl, Katie Comber.

I would like to thanks the following editors: Christine Cote, *Shanti Arts*; Kim Bridgford, *Mezzo Cammin*; Tim Holsopple, *Spindrift*; Roxana Nastase, *Scarlet Leaf Review*; Steve Glines, *Wilderness House Literary Review*; Evan Mantyk, *The Society of Classical Poets Journal*; Kathryn Jacobs, *The Road Not Taken*; Paul Brookes, *The Wombwell Rainbow*; Debra Muzikar, *The Art of Autism*, David L. O'Nan, *Fevers of the Mind*, Sean Lynch, *Serotonin*; Jane Stahl, Studio B Anthologies; Larry Robin, Moonstone Anthologies; Katie Comber, Affinity CoLab Anthologies.

I would like to thank Terry Heisey for the encouragement to publish my poetry early on. Thank you to my mother and to my children for always being willing to listen.

ABOUT THE AUTHOR

Theresa Werba the author of seven books, four in poetry: *Jesus and Eros: Sonnets, Poems and Songs* (Bardsinger Books, 2015), *Longer Thoughts* (Shanti Arts, 2020), *Sonnets* (Shanti Arts 2020) and *What Was and Is: Formal Poetry and Free Verse* (Bardsinger Books, 2024). Her work has appeared in such journals as *The Scarlet Leaf Review, The Wilderness House Literary Review, Spindrift, Mezzo Cammin, The Wombwell Rainbow, Fevers of the Mind, The Art of Autism, Serotonin, The Road Not Taken*, and the *Society of Classical Poets Journal*. Her work ranges from forms such as the ode and sonnet to free verse, with topics ranging from neurodivergence, love, loss, aging, to faith and disillusionment and more. Werba holds a Bachelor of Arts in vocal music performance from Skidmore College and a Master of Music with distinction in voice pedagogy and performance from Westminster Choir College. Werba is a member of the National Association of Teachers of Singing and has been a contributing writer for *Classical Singer* Magazine, where she has written on a myriad of topics of interest to classical singers. Her recording *Lullabies: Traditional American and International Songs* may be found on streaming services. Werba is the joyful mother of six children and grandmother to seven. Find Theresa Werba at www.bardsinger.com and on social media @thesonnetqueen.

www.ingramcontent.com/pod-product-compliance
Lightning Source LLC
Chambersburg PA
CBHW032035290426
44110CB00012B/810